LETTERS FROM SARAJEVO

Anna Cataldi is well known in Italy as a writer and journalist. As UNICEF's International Media Consultant in Sarajevo since 1992, she has frequently shared the dangers and privations of a besieged but resilient people for whom she has acted as an indefatigable emissary.

Letters from Sarajevo

VOICES OF A
BESIEGED CITY

Anna Cataldi

Translated by
Avril Bardoni

ELEMENT
Shaftesbury, Dorset ● Rockport, Massachusetts
Brisbane, Queensland

© Anna Cataldi 1993
First published in Italy as
Sarajevo: Voci da un assedio
by Baldini & Castoldi, Milan, in 1993
English translation © Avril Bardoni 1994

Published in Great Britain in 1994 by
Element Books Limited
Longmead, Shaftesbury, Dorset

Published in the USA in 1994 by
Element Inc.
42 Broadway, Rockport, MA 01966

Published in Australia in 1994 by
Element Books Limited
for Jacaranda Wiley Limited
33 Park Road, Milton, Brisbane, 4064

Cover illustration courtesy Paul Lowe, Magnum Photos Ltd
Cover design by Max Fairbrother
Design by Roger Lightfoot
Typeset by The Electronic Book Factory Ltd, Fife, Scotland
Printed and bound in Great Britain by
Redwood Books, Trowbridge, Wiltshire

British Library Cataloguing in Publication
data available

Library of Congress Cataloging in Publication
data available

ISBN 1–85230–500–2

In loving memory of my son Giovanni who died
tragically in August 1993, I dedicate this book to
every mother in Sarajevo, Moslem, Serb or Croat,
with whom I now share the same irreplaceable loss.

Anna Cataldi
November 1993

Acknowledgements

The need to make the voices of the victims of Sarajevo audible to the whole world, and the hope of helping the victims themselves, was so urgent that this book became a race against time that I would never have been able to win without the help of those whom I would now like to thank.

First of all I must thank Tanja Sekulic and Azra Mulabdic whose indispensable assistance was by no means limited to the search for and the translation of the letters.

Special thanks to Avril Bardoni for the English translation of a much expanded text that was under constant revision during the period of preparation.

In alphabetical order, but not in order of importance, I also thank:
Luigi and Daniela Bernabò, Nebojsa Bjelakovic, Mariangela Bidinotto, Zlatko Delic, Amra Foco (who has since died), Laura Fontana, Jasminka Hadziomerspahic, Sabiha Haveric, Bojana and Dragana Neskovic, Amer Hadzihasanovic, Marie Heuzè, Antioco Lostia, Emira Mulabdic, Edith Simmons, Edina Sulejmanovic, Jasmin Tanovic, UNICEF and all those who have contributed so generously by making their letters (often the only tangible link with loved ones far away and out of reach) available to me and many of whom have asked to remain unidentified.

I also thank my husband and children, and ask them to forgive me the anxiety occasioned by my visits to Sarajevo.

HVALA

Contents

Foreword
by Roy Gutman

If Sarajevo were any other European capital, the assault on civilians by men with tanks and artillery from the safety of great distance would be seen abroad as an intolerable atrocity. There would be international committees led by co-religionists or fellow nationals. People would take to the streets in protest at the siege,

That has not happened in the case of Sarajevo, and it is a mystery to those who know this unique city. At the crossroads of cultures and civilizations by virtue of its location in the middle of the Balkan peninsula, Sarajevo is open to the world. Centuries of living in close proximity moderated the religious practices of its population. Its peoples inter-married, turning Sarajevo into a truly successful melting pot. Today, because of the men with the guns sponsored by nationalists from neighbouring Serbia, a haven of tolerance is the setting for an epic struggle. Under attack in Sarajevo and in Serbia's broader war against Bosnia-Hercegovina are not merely the Muslims, Serbs, Croats, or Jews who are there by accident of birth or journey but the multi-ethnic society and the civil state.

Who in the West favours a political system organized around ethnic origin? Who, after the demise of apartheid in South Africa, would advocate installing a similar regime in Europe? Who can be a willing spectator to the extermination of a corner of civilization? In the absence of protesters marching in the streets of Washington and London, it is tempting for governments to try to duck the issues, but short-sighted, for the next generation will pay the price. Events in Sarajevo will surely affect the course of events in Europe at the start of the twenty-first century, even as they did in the first half of the twentieth.

The West has much to answer for in the unremitting siege of an almost undefended city. Opting for the course of least resistance, its governments have sent food and medicines but refused arms for legitimate self-defense. Despite the marvels of technology, they did nothing to restore telephone and postal links between Sarajevo and the outside world but were content to react to news channeled through the media.

Out of fear of being accused of censorship, several European governments, but not the United States or the United Nations, allow journalists to travel into the city on their aircraft transporting food and medicine. But under the rules of this siege, other citizens cannot see for themselves. The everyday suffering can hardly be imagined and the journalists grow numb trying to report it. Thanks to Anna Cataldi's courage in returning to Sarajevo again and again, you need not take our word for it: the letters she collected convey the authentic, unfiltered voice of Sarajevans. The ideas of a free mixing of peoples and of a civil society in which rights arise from law not from ethnic origin, are self-understood and implicit in every letter. Sarajevans are citizens of the world. Some letters convey a cry for help by those who curse their suffering. But others reveal the steel in their souls. An astonishing number of Sarajevans would sooner die defending the city and its ideals than abandon it. This is not the first assault in history, and they have reason to hope Sarajevo will endure. Poet Hussein Tahmiscic summed up the cause for hope in a 1970 essay.

The conquerers thought . . . they were eternal and forced others to believe it, only to depart one day the same way they had arrived — hurriedly . . . Those who sinned against the openness of this city, even if their way to sin was paved by good intentions, have remained constantly exposed to the judgement of time, to the derision and contempt of the following generations. No one escaped justice on the land occupied by this open city.

Introduction

'When are you going back to Italy?'

The Bosnian boy in army uniform was very pale. His lips were cracked, his clear blue eyes rimmed with red.

'In a week's time,' I replied.

'Could you do me a favour?'

A ragged scrap of paper appeared from a pocket of his trousers. He held it out to me. It bore an almost illegible telephone number.

'When you're in Italy, could you call this number?'

His English was imperfect but comprehensible.

'I could indeed, but what shall I say?'

The room in the military control-post at Kosevo Brdo, a suburb of Sarajevo, was dark. The windows were blocked with sandbags.

'You must tell them that their son Alija was killed by a grenade.'

I pulled out a notebook from my anorak pocket.

'When did he die?'

'The 17th of June. Five months ago. At ten o'clock in the morning.'

Outside, the sun shone palely on the icy silence of a winter morning. The last days of November 1992. I had come to Sarajevo a month before as a journalist assigned to cover a Unicef operation called 'A week of tranquillity'. This week, from 1–7 November, had been conceded after interminable negotiations to facilitate the distribution of clothes, medicines and food to Bosnian children 'before the winter kills them'. Of 'tranquillity' there had been none. I believe that the number of bombs that fell on Sarajevo in those seven days broke all the records for the preceding seven months.

Anyone who goes to Sarajevo has read articles, seen reports on television and assumes they are prepared for whatever they will encounter. They are mistaken. 'Sarajevo,' I was told by a journalist who had covered every war for decades, 'is the most unacceptable, the most draining, the most psychologically difficult experience that it is possible for a journalist to live through.'

I returned to Italy.

The pale Bosnian soldier had given me a wrong telephone number.

My notebook was full of other numbers, other messages, for people in Rimini, Gorizia, Düsseldorf, Milan, Vienna, Bergamo . . .

In some cases I was able to trace the person – Moslem, Serb, Croat or Jew – whose name I had been given.

Not all the messages were tragic: '. . . Tell them we're alive . . . Tell them we're fine . . .' But the message behind the words was always the same: 'Tell them that we're isolated from the rest of the world and defenceless. Tell them that we're hungry, cold and frightened, but that the desire to communicate with those we love, and the hope of seeing them again some day, lives on.'

The siege of Sarajevo took the city by surprise when, on the 6th April 1992, during a peace demonstration, forces controlled by Karadzic opened fire on the crowd from rooms 329 and 330 of the Holiday Inn hotel. That day, nobody realized that the city was already surrounded by Serbian artillery.

Sarajevo has been isolated from the world ever since.

Since 6 April 1992, from every emplacement in the mountains that sweep down in gentle curves from 2000 metres to the long, narrow valley of Sarajevo at 700 metres above sea-level, cannon, mortars, katyushas, kalashnikovs, light machine guns and snipers have been sowing death and denying the means of life.

Sarajevo, sparkling capital of Olympic Peace when the Winter Games were held there in 1984; Sarajevo, city of minarets, campanili, synagogues, a model of harmony and tolerance where people of different races and different faiths have lived, each worshipping in his own way and sharing in the life of the city for hundreds of years, has become the biggest and cruellest concentration camp in the world.

All postal communication ceased in April 1993. The telephone network has been completely down since the following June. There are no cars, buses or trams in the city, no petrol, electricity or medicines. The only food is that sent in by the aid agencies and guaranteed by the UN.

The UN troops (called UNPROFOR – United Nations PROtection FORce – in the former Yugoslavia) are based in the shell of what used to be the Post Office building, the PTT, on the other side of the new part of the city and not far from the murderous road to the airport of Butmir. Lying to the south-west of the city, on level ground unprotected by the mountains, Butmir is bombarded incessantly by all the warring factions. Hercules planes carrying aid land on the steepest dive possible and take off again – without stopping their engines – after hastily discharging the supplies that constitute a minimal life-line for the exhausted, skeletal inhabitants of Sarajevo. The only civilians who can enter and leave the city (risking their lives on the airport road, which also leads to the Ilidjza road block, the only way out of the city) are journalists accredited to UNPROFOR and aid workers belonging to the humanitarian organizations.

There are very few journalists now in Sarajevo. Sixty-two have been killed in the former Yugoslavia since January 1991, not to mention the injured, such as the young CNN reporter who will never speak again since a bullet smashed its way through her jaw, and Jean Hatzfeld, the forty-two-year-old correspondent working for *Libération* who lost one leg to a mortar shell in July 1992 and underwent twelve operations in Paris to save the remaining one, and Corinne Dufka, the Reuters photographer who, having escaped miraculously with only minor injuries when her armoured car was blown up by a land-mine, insisted on returning to work immediately.

And there are countless heroes besides. But they remain nameless because in Sarajevo assassination victims, be they doctors, nurses, aid workers, priests, UN soldiers, peace demonstrators, innocent children or helpless old people, are no longer newsworthy.

Those eye witnesses who survive return to the 'outside world' in a state of shock; they are happy to be alive, but unable to forget. So they struggle to describe their experiences, to make 'the others' understand, but find this impossible. The incidents can be described, but not the intensity, the emotion, the drama, the horror, the heroism, the purity, the continuing and inexorable injustice of an eternity made up of minutes, hours and days that can never be captured by photographs or a few minutes of satellite television.

To have been in Sarajevo is to have witnessed a tragedy, but also a miracle. The miracle is worked daily by all those who manage to 'live' in spite of everything, who cling on to their creeds and to their faith in a human dignity that retains its humanity even in inhuman conditions. Only if one has been in Sarajevo can one understand that, however much one suffers for and with these people, the truth about this tragic folly can only be told by those who are involved in it and have no way out.

This is why I began to collect letters written by the besieged people of Sarajevo.

The first victim of a war is time, the passage of time marked out by the seasons. So I decided to group the letters by season. This posed many problems. In fact, letters written during the spring and summer of 1992 were almost non-existent, as the inhabitants of Sarajevo, like those of any other busy modern city, were no longer in the habit of writing them. They used the phone instead, and until the middle of June 1992 the telephones were still working.

Later, the bombardments that took place in the summer were so brutal that no one imagined that the rest of the world would stand by and allow a massacre of such proportions to continue. Only in the autumn did the desperate reality of the siege and the abandonment of Sarajevo by the rest of the world, strike home in all its daily, inescapable horror.

The second victim of a war is the sense of reality. This is why I decided to preface each season's letters with a brief chronology of the so-called 'historical' events of the period. History comprises the dates, the events one reads about in the paper. The letters are the eternity of non-events, the desperate waiting, the nullity, the wear and tear of dimensionless time. Only the victims of the war can know that the waiting is sometimes worse than the killing.

The chronology is the siege from the 'outside'; the letters are the 'inside'.

How many truces, how many cease-fires have been agreed? How many Peace Conferences have taken place in the various capitals of a badly-informed western Europe, feeding hopes destined to disappointment? How many promises of help have been made? How many threats of armed intervention to stop this genocide that is being perpetrated 'live' in the full glare of world-wide satellite television?

And in the meantime people continue to die in Sarajevo, killed by snipers' bullets, shell-fire, hunger, cold, madness, illness or simple desperation.

But people also continue to write in Sarajevo. Bombs may be falling all around them, but by the light of oil lamps, in the damp, cold cellars, adults, children, university professors, housewives, intellectuals, soldiers and labourers write letters whose chances of reaching their destination are seldom more than precarious. Cast like bread upon the waters, entrusted to anybody, even a complete stranger, who is able to leave the besieged city, stuffed into haversacks or into the pockets of chance travellers, and posted 'outside' to uncertain destinations (refugees' addresses tend to have only short-term validity), many letters are lost.

All the letters in this book are authentic, though quite a few names have been altered to protect the privacy of the recipients and, in some cases, the safety of the senders. The translation was not easy. It was made possible by Tanja Sekulic and Azra Mulabdic. I knew no Serbo-Croat, and their Italian was limited. I knew little of their traditions, customs and faiths. However, I shared with the besieged correspondents our knowledge of a situation so terrible that for Tanja and Azra, who had grown up in Sarajevo in peacetime, it was all but impossible to grasp.

Each of us contributed what we knew. We were united by the determination to render faithfully this chorus of suffocated voices rising from all ethnic groups, ages and cultures, and carry its cry to the four corners of the earth:

'Help us! We too have the right to live!'

Anna Cataldi
Sarajevo, December 1993

LETTERS FROM SARAJEVO

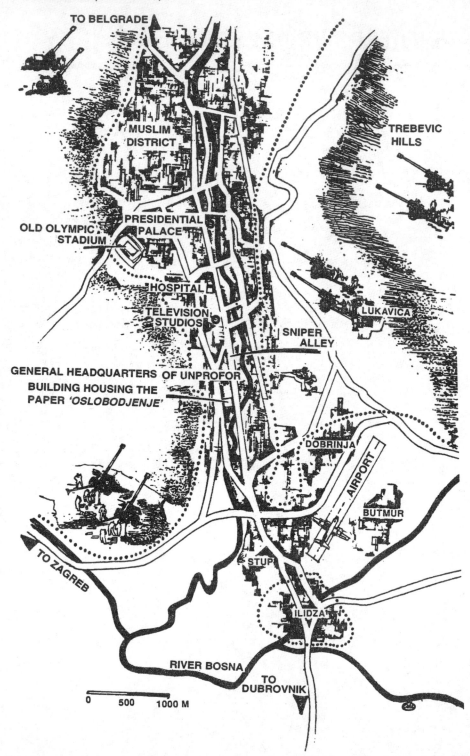

TO BELGRADE

MUSLIM
DISTRICT

TREBEVIC
HILLS

OLD OLYMPIC
STADIUM

PRESIDENTIAL
PALACE

LUKAVICA

HOSPITAL

TELEVISION
STUDIOS

SNIPER
ALLEY

GENERAL HEADQUARTERS OF UNPROFOR
BUILDING HOUSING THE
PAPER 'OSLOBODJENJE'

DOBRINJA

AIRPORT

BUTMUR

STUP

TO ZAGREB

ILIDZA

RIVER BOSNA

TO
DUBROVNIK

0   500   1000 M

Sarajevo surrounded by Serbian gun-batteries

Spring 1992

My city was beautiful
this city on the banks of a river
my city was beautiful
and gave joy to all who lived there . . .

February 28 – March 1
Referendum organized by the government of Bosnia-Hercegovina to establish independence from the Federal Socialist Republic of Yugoslavia. Sixty-six per cent of citizens vote for an independent Bosnia-Hercegovina. In a former plebiscite of Serbian nationals organized by the SDS (Serbian Democratic Party), ninety per cent had voted for Bosnia-Hercegovina to remain part of Yugoslavia.

March 27
An initiative of the Serbian Democratic Party establishes the Republic of Bosnia-Hercegovina.

April 4–5
First armed clashes in Sarajevo.

April 5
Peace demonstration in Sarajevo. Serb militiamen fire on the demonstrators.

April 6
Demonstrations continue outside the parliament building. Serbian snipers disperse the crowd. The EC officially recognizes the independence of Bosnia-Hercegovina.

April 7
The United States recognizes the independence of Bosnia-Hercegovina (together with that of Slovenia and Croatia).

April 8
The government of Bosnia-Hercegovina proclaims a state of emergency. Throughout the month Sarajevo is bombarded by Serbian troops occupying strategic positions overlooking the city and having at their disposal a vast quantity of arms from the arsenals of the Jugoslav Federal Army (JNA) and the Territorial Defence (TO).

April 27
Serbia and Montenegro proclaim the Federal Republic of Yugoslavia.

May 2
The JNA sides with the Serb militia. Their combined forces destroy the postal communications building in Sarajevo and other essential installations.

May 14
The first allegations of 'ethnic cleansing' in the former Yugoslavia are made by the State Department of the United States of America.

May 22
Bosnia-Hercegovina becomes a member of the UN.

May 27
The 'Bread Queue Massacre' in Vase Miskin street. All the victims are civilians.

May 30
The building housing the newspaper *Oslobodjenje* is subjected to a violent bombardment.

Sarajevo, 22 April 1992

My great and adored friend,

Today is Wednesday. I am sitting on the floor listening to the grenades.* Very interesting. Every time I think about those idiots behind them I want to be sick. Outside the sun is shining and primulas and dandelions are in flower. No birds are singing. Or possibly they are but we can't hear them. It really is stupid of me to be writing you this letter.
   In the first place:

1. There is no post and who knows if you will ever receive it;
2. I don't know what to say because too many things are happening here and they are all equally interesting.

   I hope these two excuses are enough to persuade you to overlook my stupidity (the sovereign quality, indivisible and open to every nationality . . .)

Lada**

---

*Bombs, mortars, shells, all kinds of explosive devices – as opposed to bullets – have become known generically in Sarajevo as 'grenades'.
**Further letters from Lada, a girl in her late teens to her friend appear on pages 14, 15, 19, 34, 36, 43, 94.

Sarajevo, 24 April 1992

Love,

Friday. I tried to phone you earlier today but couldn't get through.

I'm in a weird state of mind. Madness is closing in on me little by little, and is, I feel, going to be very difficult to shake off. I don't know how long I can bear this madness. This evening, I have decided, I am going to get drunk with some friends (super people) who live in the same building, hoping it'll make me forget all this for a while at least.

At the moment I am listening to 'The girls in their light summer dresses'.

Here is some 'second-hand' information:

1. A member of our 'society' known to the masses as D. P. has been spotted in the ranks of the so-called Serbian territorials. He's now in the building opposite and I find this rather cheering, though I don't know why;

2. Yesterday evening the 'companions' from the house over the way (Serbian paramilitaries) were out in the garden clanking bottles and singing (and murdering) the song that goes:

. . . and in the woods, beside the ancient trunk,
a hand caresses yours . . .
the time of golden dreams has come,
good night . . .

and then they went to bed.
I know it seems impossible, but it happened. Complete insanity.

Lada

Sarajevo, Sunday 24 April 1992

Me again. Today everything is quiet. Probably because it's Easter. I went into the centre of town yesterday, and it was lovely. Mirela said that Vase Miskin Street was just like Stradun in Dubrovnik! These last few days there have been so many people out and about in our city, particularly in the town centre, that you could really think you were walking along Stradun. It's seven o'clock in the evening now, and dusk is falling slowly. The weather is wonderful. There are summer smells in the air. I just can't tell you how fed up I am with having to stay shut up indoors. It's ghastly. Now I'm terribly depressed and don't know what to do with myself. What I'd like to do more than anything else is climb the hill and look down on the city in the valley. And then up at the sky. Dear oh dear, what a romantic!

I used to think this shit would never get me down. The worst of it is the uncertainty and no one knowing or even being able to imagine what is going to happen. Hey, baby, I long to write to you and tell you all about it, but what I've written so far seems only stupid and unreal. I'm going . . . to smoke a cigarette.

With love,
Lada

I'm back again, I'm back again,
better than before
never . . . ever, where is the gang now
that never, ever stopped?
Where's the gang, where's the fun
and games . . . blah . . . blah . . . blah.

Outside the sun's still shining. And while it lasts, so does the ceasefire (I'm glad to say). People get along. Everything gets along. Even I get along with strong, sweet-smelling grappa, while disco music gets along with Mtv. You, in that faraway country, are getting along with Italian like a dragon. Little one, this grappa is already starting to 'go to my head', and I would love . . . but I don't know . . .

Mirela and Marko have split up because he was saying shitty things about the war. Serbia — but you know it already — what shit!

I do like this music on Mtv! Now some blacks are singing a song about Tennessee. You know, I wouldn't half mind being there at the moment.

Baby, I love you lots, believe me or not.

Lada

Sarajevo, 10 May 1992

My dear son,

The situation here has continued to deteriorate since the day you all left. I thank God that you, your wife and my grandson have been able to get away to safety.

I am sending you this 'open letter' because I should like our Italian friends and all the world to know what is happening in our city.

I used to have a dear friend at *Il Giornale* in Milan. I would like you to pass this letter on to him as he might be able to arrange for its publication.

Sarajevo, May 1992

To the Editor of *Il Giornale*
Dear Sir,

I am writing to you, as a doyen of Italian journalism, from the ruins of a beautiful and unique city – Sarajevo – which, though now devastated in the most barbaric fashion, was once, as your authoritative paper described it, 'the picturesque Jerusalem of the Balkans'.

And now there is nothing here, my dear sir, but an inferno of death, a stench of burning, hunger, tears, men dead and mutilated, mosques, churches and synagogues wrecked, libraries, nursery schools, hotels, museums, residential areas all reduced to heaps of rubble . . . In short, a city damned, like dozens of other cities of my native Hercegovina, ravaged and occupied.

In this chaos of death and destruction that has already lasted forty days, I have learned by roundabout means that your own paper, *Il Giornale*, has been one of the foremost in the struggle to obtain the truth about this inferno where the Serbian soldiery, the army and bands of Serbian mercenaries are killing my fellow citizens mercilessly with heavy artillery and missiles, destroying my besieged city, laying waste my country.

I beg you, personally, out of compassion for the pain and sacrifice of so many innocent victims, to allow me to communicate my feelings to the Italian people.

I am truly ashamed of having been ingenuous enough to believe, during the last four years when I was serving as consul general of the former Socialist Federal Republic of Yugoslavia in Milan, that I was representing a country and a set of values to which the atavism of the leaders and nationalistic planners of Belgrade was completely foreign and immaterial.

I am ashamed of having been a member of political bodies that so ably concealed the long-term designs for Milosevic's 'greater Serbia' and the army, thus hiding, in truly diabolical fashion, the real objective of the whole struggle.

I am ashamed of being present at a time and a place (May 1992, Sarajevo) where, at the end of the twentieth century and upon European territory, children are killed with precision rifles, innocent men with mortars, where aeroplanes are dropping bombs and where, to put it briefly, every living thing, everything human and everything that exists is being destroyed with the utmost brutality.

I am ashamed of having wasted time and energy, during the eight wonderful years I spent as a diplomat first in Rome and later in Milan, trying to acquaint my Italian friends with the culture and civilisation of my homeland instead of evaluating more realistically and thus combating all the indications that a policy of genocide would inevitably result from that barbaric 'Plan for Greater Serbia'.

I am ashamed of the powerlessness I share with nearly all my fellow-citizens and fellow-countrymen, and of my inability to oppose the Serbian bandits and what was once Tito's army with anything more than silent disdain and disgust.

I am ashamed of showing, like all my fellow-citizens, such weakness in the face of the aggressors and murderers, even to the point of watching, in silence and without opposition, as they counted the bodies of dead children, and helplessly watching scenes of horror in Brcko, Bijeljina, Foca, Mostar, Zvornik, Bosanski Brod, Capljina, Siroki Brijeg and other cities in Bosnia and Hercegovina, where the corpses of innocent people lay with their throats cut, and whole villages were burnt and destroyed.

I am ashamed of the lack of conscience shown by the intellectuals and journalists in Belgrade who, blind and deaf to the crimes, the destruction and the pillage of my devastated country, say nothing.

I am ashamed of Europe for remaining silent for too long and for not making decisions.

This is why I am begging you, my dear sir, to continue with your noble mission of revealing the truth and appealing to the consciences of all those who should, like me, be ashamed of this European tragedy.

Dr. Aziz Hadzihasanovic
former Consul General of the
former Republic of Yugoslavia

Sarajevo, today is Saturday, the 16th of the month of May in the year 1992

Here I am,

They are fighting their war and our little lives mean absolutely nothing to them. I'm well, I'm still in one piece, etc . . . And the same goes for my family. I'm a bit hysterical, a bit jittery, but that's hardly surprising after spending four days in the entrance hall in front of the lift with hopes that this shit will ever end growing fainter and fainter. Yesterday they set fire to the building next door. We were fired on by tanks. Can you imagine how upsetting all this is? If you get in the way of one of those 'infernal machines' you've had it. I saw it drive in one side of the building and out the other, trailing the windows, frames and all, and not forgetting the curtains. There's a window lying all by itself now, twenty metres away from the building. Wonderful! So the people living in the bombed building had to escape and somehow manage to get into our entrance hall, because exactly half of them no longer have a home. They slept with us last night. We played the hosts on the grand scale, giving them the best places in the cellar. It was a bit of a squash but, as you know, we stick together.

And the guns are at it again today. Milosevic and Karadzic had agreed to bomb our native city – or what's left of it – between them. One of the generals apparently got a bit rebellious yesterday, so we weren't bombed, which doesn't mean they won't do it again in the future. All I shall say is that these bombs are being used in defiance of the regulations, and rather than my filling up page after page telling you what's going on, you can read up about it somewhere else. I managed to discover a bit about the effect they have, and I assure you it's very disturbing.

Rock'n'Roll, discos etc . . . There's been no electricity for three days, so I can't go to a disco. I don't know what's happening. Half the city is without power, so I can't get any information about anything. I don't even know if the radio and TV stations are working, but I doubt it. I heard that the relay station had been hit. I don't know whether it's true, but why shouldn't it be? Even our batteries are flat. We can't even listen to the news on the radio. This is driving me mad. Not in my wildest dreams could I have imagined this shit. It is sheer, sheer hell. I no longer wonder if I shall stay sane, but only if I shall survive. This is one big turd, and damn it all, I've actually forgotten how people express themselves. And so I really don't know what else I can tell you, because if I could describe the horror that's thumping away inside me, a ferocious monster, slimy, skinless and filthy, would come crawling out of the paper . . .

Bye for now, little one, I'll write again when (with God's help) I feel more myself!

I miss you ever so much,
Lada

Milan, 18 May 1992

Dear Professor Popov,

I have been having dreams continually ever since I returned. I dream that I am still in Sarajevo. But then I wake up and find myself in Milan. I was indeed in Sarajevo two weeks ago.

Sarajevo remains embedded in my consciousness in the form of six scenes, and before they fade away I want to record them and should like you to read them:

Milan, 10 May. I have just put the phone down:
'My daughter, I am well. There is no glass in the windows, and the building opposite has a gaping hole in it. We are alive and in one piece. We were even able to buy some bread today. Do not worry about us!'

Only a short conversation, but it gives me a moment of relief because I have learnt that they are well. They are alive and in one piece.

I have been to Sarajevo. I am now back in Milan and do not have to worry about whether my son will have a mug of milk tomorrow or not. I went to Sarajevo despite being warned by everybody, even before April 6th, not to go. I refused to believe them. But I'm glad I went because now I understand many things. I saw how they lied to us, robbed us, destroyed our homes, forced us to die of starvation, refused to allow us to work, wounded and killed us, and all this to make us believe that we hate each other and cannot live together. I saw how they were even capable of firing at a crowd in front of the Parliament building. These people, sick to death of the nationalists, had gathered, unarmed, to overthrow their power, the power of those who were, by contrast, armed to the teeth. I understood that they have not succeeded in turning us, the common people, into nationalists.

As I write, the scenes flood back into my mind:

Scene 1

It is Friday 27 March. As we wait in Belgrade for our flight to Sarajevo, we are watching the news on Channel One of RTV Belgrade. The first fifteen minutes consists of a speech by the

Serbian president about the Serbian railway system. And at that very moment Bosanski Brod is going up in flames. Then comes a report on the founding of the Serbian Republic of Bosnia-Hercegovina. Leers on the smug faces of the warmongers. The refinery in Bosanski Brod has been hit, but the news merits no more than a couple of words. We are very frightened as we board our plane, and as we fly towards Sarajevo we wonder if we will be met by barricades. I have a strange sensation of flying into a trap. And another, even stranger sensation, that I don't mind.

Scene 2

The first days in Sarajevo pass with every appearance of normality. There is a state of anarchy. I study the faces of the people. I wonder what they are thinking, and what they are capable of doing. The streets are overrun with black marketeers. There is tension in the air.

Scene 3

It all started on 5 April. We went down to the shelter for the first time. They are fighting one against the other, 'two Moslem streets and two Serbian streets with the help of a skyscraper'; Serb paramilitaries have occupied the Republic's police training school in the Vrace district. First close encounter with a grenade: the feeling of helplessness while you wait to see where it will drop is almost unbearable. But you get used to it.

The lies, the disinformation, the reciprocal accusations begin to pour out as if the events themselves were not horrible enough already. The Moslems are unarmed, and have no means of defending themselves. Paraga remains in Busovaca. Serbian heavy artillery is destroying Kupres. Listica is being bombed. Serb paramilitaries pound the city of Visegrad with mortar and fire. That chauvinist, half-mad criminal Sabanovic has threatened to blow up the hydro-electric dam at Visegrad to stop the Serbian aggression. And then there's . . . Foca, Zvornik . . .

One incident sparks off another. Ordinary people, laden with baggage of all kinds, are escaping to any place that seems to offer a measure of safety. Families of mixed Serbs and Moslems say farewell and split up in the belief that they will be safer if each is 'with his own'. This is precisely what 'they' wanted.

We are being made to suffer.

Grenades fall upon Sarajevo. If the shelling stops, snipers take over. Yet no one has a placard on his back saying 'Serb' or 'Moslem' or 'Croat' . . . All they can do is repeat the worn-out old phrase that the end justifies the means.

The firing continues, the trams run, the bakers bake their bread, journalists and doctors no longer have time to go home. The city rebels against the war that has been forced upon it and puts on a brave face.

The Serb units do not select their targets. They destroy hospitals, residential areas. Their reasoning seems to be: 'You wanted independence, now we'll show you what it means!'

They do not even care about the one hundred and fifty thousand Serbs and Montenegrins shut up in the shelters with no milk for their children.

All that matters to them is that the members of the Serb Nationalist Party should have found a safe place for themselves and their families. Aleksa Buha, professor of philosophy and 'Minister for Foreign Affairs of the Serbian Republic of Bosnia-Hercegovina' is in Novi Sad. 'Ministers' Maksimovic and Ostojic are in Foca, beyond the range of mortars.

The whereabouts of Karadzic are unknown. He may be in Pale.*

Scene 4

This is how the events unfolded:

A demonstration in front of the Parliament building. A vast tide of people rolls towards the city. The miners from Breza, Kakanj and Vares arrive, then people from Mostar, Zenica and Tuzla. Men confront the nationalists' banners with anything – the Yugoslavian flag, photographs of Marshall Tito – they have been able to lay their hands on. Not out of nostalgia or any desire to return to the old ways, but only because there are no new icons.

---

*Pale: A city in the mountains above Sarajevo, seat of government of the self-styled Serbian Republic of Bosnia-Hercegovina.

The ex-communists try to manipulate the demonstrators. Serb snipers fire into the crowd. The president, Alija Izetbegovic, arrives to make a speech; he is given two minutes' grace before the whistling starts. The report on Croat TV can be summed up in one sentence: 'There is no interest in anything Yugoslavian,' they said.

The ploy had been obvious for some time already. President Tudjman has achieved his aim of shifting the war into Bosnia and strengthening his position in western Hercegovina in a media blackout. The SDA (Izetbegovic's Party of Democratic Action) issues a communiqué severely criticizing 'the manipulation of the people'. The SDS (Karadzic's Serbian Democratic Party) accuses Izetbegovic of having incited the people to revolt. The Yugoslavian army says one thing and does another.

The people still cannot bring themselves to believe (though they will have to very soon, unfortunately) that the guns on the tanks and the mortars of the soldiers were trained upon them, but were still hoping, on the contrary, that the army would protect them.

Beneath a rain of bullets from the snipers, with no one capable of organizing the revolt and enforcing its demands, the demonstrators dispersed.

These were their demands:

1. The dissolution of the Government.
2. The formation of a Government they could trust.
3. New elections immediately.

The demands were so much wasted effort. What happened outside Parliament laid bare the very nub of the whole situation, which is that the nationalists will never reach any sort of agreement, simply because they do not want it. It is now also clear that peace can never be re-established in Bosnia-Hercegovina. Events have moved on too far.

Scene 5

We are returning to Milan, I feel sick at heart, ashamed because I am leaving. I try to convince myself that there are ample reasons for justifying this decision.

The scene at the airport recalls films of Vietnam or Beirut.

In the plane, people are even sitting on the floor, each with a child upon his or her knee. At Belgrade Airport they enter our names in a register. They count the refugees, recording their addresses as well. The official looks surprised when we tell him that we are returning home, to Milan. He sees something not to his liking. He has realized from our names that my husband and I are from different ethnic groups, groups that should be hating each other, not living together.

We spend the night in Belgrade. We watch a two-hour programme on television about Arkan and the 'liberation' of Osijek in Croatia. They speak about 'cleansing' the shelters with bombs. I remember the boys and girls in our shelter in Sarajevo: five Serb-Montenegrin families, three Moslem and two Croatian who were all keeping each others' spirits up and helping each other survive this madness. Rage and impotence surge up inside me. The presenter, a smartly-dressed woman, puts polite questions to her guest.

Scene 6

The end of the journey. We arrive in Zürich, and find the cleanliness, orderliness and peacefulness of Switzerland almost offensive. The prettiness of the landscape, the opulence that seems to ooze from it, suddenly reveals the images in our minds for what they really are: an absurdity.

How many men are fighting in Bosnia? A hundred and fifty thousand? Two hundred thousand? Two hundred and fifty thousand? They have taken hostage the entire Bosnian population.

My dear Professor, how I should like to know what the state presidents of the former Yugoslavia are dreaming about these days, and whether their dreams are anything like mine.

Because the devil has entered my house.

And I have drawn a vast circle on the floor and want to drag all my loved ones into the circle with me. But they don't believe me and refuse to come in. So I cry out because I cannot protect them.

Professor, I have seen the devil very clearly and I have recognized him.

But sooner or later even he will be judged.

Your one-time student
Tatjana Sekulic

Sarajevo, 29 May 1992

My far-away children,

You will have read in the papers what happened here two days ago. We thought that by now we had seen the worst, but what happened in Miskin Street is something I cannot describe, something for which I can find no words. My friend, Professor Zdravko Grebo, spoke on the radio station B-92 on 27 May. I made a note of what he said.

'Friends of Sarajevo, I did not go once to see what had happened in Miskin Street. I went four times. The first was at half past ten. Then I went back to the radio station to broadcast an appeal: blood was needed for those many, many people who were dying. I returned to the scene and saw A. P. and Z. H., the two best-known of the Sarajevo commanders, unable to speak, weeping in desperation. A short while ago I went back again, carrying in my car people who wanted to donate their blood.

And I am now speaking to you from the studios of independent radio. Yes, I was in Miskin Street, but not right at the beginning; I arrived half an hour after hearing the news. If you want an eye-witness account of the scene, I cannot give it to you, it is not possible to describe it . . . Because there is no rational explanation on earth that can account for what has happened in Sarajevo during the last ten hours, not even in terms of implementing fascist and imperialistic policies.

You my listeners will already have heard – or perhaps not, even my memory is numbed – of yesterday's severe bombing of the maternity clinic 'Zehra Muhidovic', right next door to the trauma clinic where most of Sarajevo's wounded are treated.

This carnage was, we thought, the furthest point to which madness could reach, and that no mentality, even the most disturbed, could conceive of anything worse. So this morning, a beautiful spring morning, there was an aura almost of tranquillity. And a large number of people plucked up their courage and gathered outside the only bakery still open in our city.

People actually crawled out of their shelters and stood in a queue. And then, in a single cluster, the grenades fell on them. Over a hundred people were badly injured and the total of dead has risen to thirty as I speak. Vase Miskin Street . . .'

As a lesson to the inhabitants of Sarajevo who had dared to come out of hiding, to walk in the streets, to demonstrate the fact that they were not afraid even though the men positioned on the slopes of Mount Trebevic could see them with the naked eye . . . All is ruin, devastation, destruction . . . I don't know what to say. Rivers of blood were flowing down Miskin Street, and that is neither 'poetic licence' nor a metaphor!

This wasn't a case of the splashes of blood to which we are becoming accustomed. In Miskin Street the blood literally flowed! Arms and legs landed on balconies . . . a woman clutching her own leg in her arms tries to escape, God knows where to . . . men roll down the street like logs . . . a woman sits cradling her two sons, one of four and the other of seven, both dead . . .

Each scene more heartbreaking than the last . . . ! If anyone doubts that this really happened, it has all been recorded by Sarajevo television, and if the world still has a conscience, it should transmit these pictures, just as they are. Sarajevo television offers them to the whole world, including the television networks here that once knew the meaning of collaboration. I ask nothing more. Only that public opinion in Belgrade and Serbia should know what happened, that people should see Miskin Street transformed into a river of blood for themselves. I have seen terrible things . . . an entire grenade in a man's stomach . . .

I truly do not know what else has to happen in Sarajevo and Bosnia-Hercegovina before those who will not hear are convinced that Fascism is at the gates and are stung into action.

Once more I beg you . . . then I will ask nothing more. I shall stay here to defend this city . . .

MAY GOD FORBID THAT THE FATE FORESHADOWED BY BLOOD-SOAKED MISKIN STREET SHOULD EVER BECOME REALITY!

My dear children, I feel unable to say more.

I send you my very dear love,
your father

Sarajevo, 30 May 1992

My dear Olga,

It is truly dreadful that I should have to send you my sympathy like this on the death of your daughter. It hardly seems possible that times are such that our generation must bury its own children.

I remember Bentbasa and our graduation ceremony. You invited me to your house afterwards for a cup of coffee. I pleaded a family engagement and said: 'I'll come some other time'.

Well, this is 'some other time'. But did it really have to be so sad?

I heard the news last night from my cousin who was a friend of your daughter's. I screamed. I have no idea if anyone heard my scream; it was something horrible, primitive. I can't believe that the 'men' who come from elsewhere have no love for this city of ours. I cannot believe that on the very road to the Drvenija bridge that we used to walk along on our way to school, they should now be killing our children as they go in search of bread with their poor little plastic bags.

Night after night I lie awake thinking, trying to imagine these creatures (I cannot call them 'men') who are shelling our city.

Do you remember those times in our cellar when we shared our black bread with peanut butter and corn syrup with them? We were all equal.

Why did we ever allow them to come? Why did we allow them to study with us, graduate with us – without, however, absorbing our way of thinking and our tolerance?

For centuries Sarajevo has practised a tolerance for which Latinluk, Taslihan and Mahala* are true metaphors.

I read that they are destroying everything.

Can they destroy 'everything'?

That I do not believe.

I am more optimistic than when I spoke to Igor . . . For all of you, too, who have remained in Sarajevo, choosing not to leave your native city.

---

*The three oldest districts in Sarajevo, where all races and religions – Catholic, Moslem, Orthodox – have lived in harmony for centuries.

My dear, anything I can say by way of consolation is probably useless. A pain such as yours is, they say, the greatest one can experience, far worse than the pain of childbirth.

The time will come when we can meet again, when we citizens of Sarajevo can once more look one another in the face in spite of all that Andric** wrote about bells and clock-towers, in spite of everything.

I assure you of my love for you and for all your family, and my thoughts are constantly with you.

Yours,
Merima

This letter was written after the 'Bread Queue Massacre' by a Moslem woman born in Sarajevo to her Serbian friend whose daughter was killed in Miskin Street on 27 May 1992.

**Ivo Andric (1892–1975), winner of the 1961 Nobel Prize for Literature. Born in Travnik, and of deeply pro-Serbian leanings, he once wrote: '. . . listening to all the diverse and desperate summons of the bells of Sarajevo, I decided that I could no longer remain in my adoptive homeland . . . Bosnia is a country of hate and fear'.

Summer 1992

WHEN DADDY IS FIGHTING IN THE WAR

If only you knew how it feels
when your daddy is fighting in the war
you run away from unhappiness, but unhappiness follows you
you hear no news of your father
and one day, when everything is getting black
Daddy knocks on the door
stays for five days
and then happiness goes away again
and my heart beats loudly like a little clock
and now I cannot write any more because my daddy
is not here, close beside me.

Zana, aged 12

June
The Federal Army officially announces its 'retreat' from Bosnia-Hercegovina. Most of its men and equipment, however, are turned over to the Serbian forces. The roads and communications systems in Sarajevo are being systematically destroyed. Water and power supplies are interrupted for the first time.

8 June
The UN passes Resolution No. 758 enabling it to send observers to guarantee the security of Sarajevo's Butmir airport, which is to be used for landing humanitarian aid.

28 June
President Mitterand of France arrives in Sarajevo.
The UN votes on Resolution No. 761 putting the airport at Sarajevo under the jurisdiction of the blue berets for the humanitarian aid operation.

July
Water and power in Sarajevo are both cut off.
The International Red Cross reports on the existence of concentration camps in Bosnia-Hercegovina.

13 July
The number of UN troops in Sarajevo rises to 1,600.

27 July
Telephonic communication between Sarajevo and the outside world ceases totally.

28 July
One hundred women and children are flown to Milan under the auspices of the Comune di Milano (Milanese local authority) and the Children's Embassy.

5 August
The United States asks for the collaboration of all UN member states in the gathering of information relating to war crimes in Bosnia-Hercegovina.

14 August
The UN names Tadeusz Mazowiecki head of the commission investigating violations of civil rights in the former Yugoslavia.

25 August
Lord Carrington resigns as mediator for the former Yugoslavia.

26 August
An international conference on the situation in the former Yugoslavia opens in London under the joint auspices of the UN and EC.

28 August
Vijecnica, the Sarajevo National Library, is hit and burnt to the ground. More than 100,000 books of inestimable value are destroyed.

Throughout the whole period, journalists on Sarajevo radio and TV and the daily newspaper *Oslobodjenje*, continue to work.

Radio and television programmes are broadcast from the reinforced basements of RTV, a building that is constantly under Serbian artillery and sniper fire. The policy of multi-ethnic teams of journalists is unchanged. Many journalists are killed while fulfilling their assignments.

3 September
The Geneva Conference begins under the auspices of the UN.
An Italian military aircraft carrying blankets to Sarajevo is shot down. All four members of the crew are killed.

Sarajevo, 22 June 1992

Happy birthday to you!

I'm thinking about you, etc. etc. and I'm glad you're not here today. Because it would be daft to have a birthday party when the Chetniks* might start blazing away at any moment and wreck everything. It would be nice to be somewhere near the sea now, drinking wine, eating cheese and pastries.
    There's something strange in the air today.
    The sky is blue and it feels just like the start of the summer holidays, except that we don't go to school now and where we used to play in the street outside, Chetnik beards now poke round the corner.
    I think that's it. I haven't heard from you for ages (two days).
    I don't know what to do with myself. I would love a beer, but there isn't any beer in Sarajevo. There's nothing I can do about it, and I'm still thirsty.
    But I must stop now. I wish you happiness and long life, I hope you have a happy day today, I love you, give me a call, and forgive me, but my head's in a bit of a whirl.
    Happy birthday!

Lada

---

*Chetniks: Serbian combatants with a well-earned reputation for outstanding brutality.

Sarajevo, 3 July 1992

Dear Pasa,

I can't tell you how happy your letter made me, and how much it meant to me. I thought you had forgotten me, but your letter proved me wrong. The first thing I would beg you to do is call Stana and tell her that we are all well. Tell her to kiss my adored Armin a thousand times for me and tell him that his Auntie loves him more than anything else in the world and thinks about him all the time. I am so glad that your parents are with you, and Boris too, because it's better you should all be together. I would give anything to see Armin and Stana. I can't tell you how much I miss them. I was so sorry that Ajs and Nera had to stay behind, because your dogs are also part of the family.

Your mother will, I am sure, have told you how I felt after your departure. I'm much better now although I have had two very narrow escapes from grenades. Our neighbourhood has changed so much and our life is so different now. I could go on for hours about this. Most days follow a set pattern. I try to get out for a while in the morning, then I have some lunch, with boiled macaroni or rice (even you would manage to lose weight if you were here). I do some knitting and then sit in the café until nine. Then home and bed. Tell Stana that I cannot leave the city. Alija can't, as a soldier, and I couldn't leave him alone.

Tell Aco how distressed I am about his father. I was so fond of him. He wept on the balcony when we were thrown out of Grbavica. I shall never forget that. He came out onto the balcony, waved to me, and tears were rolling down his cheeks. You can't imagine how I suffered at that moment. I haven't been able to contact any of your friends, but I shall go on trying, and let you know how I get on in my next letter. I can't think of anything else to tell you. I shall try, if I can, to call you on the satellite phone. It won't be easy.

Give my love to everyone. I shall stay in this accursed city hoping, as you say, that God exists for me too, and that one day we shall meet again.

Melika

Sarajevo, 31 July 1992

Me again as usual,

From the date you might think I have been lazy and not written to you for ages. But appearances can be deceptive. I don't know what's going on in my head, but I'm just not up to writing. Or rather, I can write but I don't know what to write about. Everything I told you about in my last letter just goes on going on. Every day is the same as the one before. Every day is so like the one before that I no longer know what day of the week it is. Here in Sarajevo time seems to have lost its meaning. We're living in a different age, a weird and distant age that we have to get used to or go mad.

I'm still 'hanging on'. I get on with things, I won't give in to depression. The days seem to drag by interminably, while the months flash past and you can't even tell one from the other. It'll soon be August and that means more problems.

When all's said and done we're only a small Balkan country in the throes of a bloody and disgusting war. (You probably can't even imagine the hair-raising things that go on here. Nor could I if I had not seen them with my own eyes. And how I wish I hadn't!) And Europe and America don't give a toss about this bloody war. Everything they say is so much hot air, and after all the help they promised they've done NOTHING! You may not understand what's going on, but truly dirty games are being played here in which our unimportant little lives mean nothing at all. All this is a colossal shit!

You know, there are still a lot of people here who believe that the 'Great Powers' are going to come to their rescue, but the truth is that they won't lift a finger. People cling to their illusions because that makes everything more bearable, but they are all lies.

You know, baby, we can't possibly win without a miracle. I feel as if I were struggling to survive in a slaughterhouse in the hope that a miracle will save me from the hands of an evil and merciless butcher.

Sometimes I laugh about it all and say the stupidest things. And my brother, meanwhile, is fighting in the front line at Mojmilo.

My fiancé is also fighting at the front, at Borko, where the Jewish cemetery is, as you know. They are both fighting for our native city. At the moment I am living in the Alipasino Polje district, known as Fase-C. I had to move into a house belonging to other people for reasons of mental health. It's a long story, but provides yet more proof of how shitty things can get. My parents returned to Mojmilo. The firing gets heavier every day and mamma and papa have to run across that big stretch of grass between Mojmilo and Fase-C every day just trusting to luck. Two men were killed at that very spot only a few days ago. When things like this happen people lose their nerve for the next three hours, then go back to using the same path as if nothing had happened. It's the only way to survive. It seems ridiculous to expose oneself to danger in order to stay alive, but that's how it is. Because this too is a way of fighting.

You know, baby, it infuriates the Chetniks to see people going to work in the middle of town while they have the city under siege. I believe it's driving them mad. Every day there's a new obscenity. People are killed. Every ten days there's a massacre like the one in Vase Miskin street, though on a lesser scale. The television has stopped showing these incidents (even they can't get everywhere as they used to) but they're reported on the radio as if they were something quite normal. 'A grenade fell today' – or two or three, the number's unimportant – 'in Tito Street, killing fifteen people and injuring eight' etc. It all sounds appalling, but one gets used to it.

But as for me, these things still turn my stomach, so I don't listen to the news. What I see with my own eyes is quite enough – too much, in fact – but I can't go around with my eyes closed. We have to resign ourselves to everything that's happening. Bugger it all. The war has become our routine, our daily bread, our way of life.

Even I have learnt a lot of important things about life in these last months. But that's another story. Perhaps I've only learnt to accept things as they are without crapping about it so much. I don't know. I've grown up and become more responsible (I know that sounds ridiculous), but I can still crap about it.

And now for the rest of the news (a bit late) that I forgot to tell you when I saw you.

Mirko was peppered with grapeshot during the fight for Dobrinja. That's really stale news and I believe he has now completely recovered. Besides, he wasn't seriously injured.

Paja was wounded, in the leg I believe. That's also rather stale news. Now for something more recent.

Mira and Amir are fine. I saw them a few days ago.

Sima Glavosevic was wounded in the face by a piece of shrapnel during the fighting for Dobrinja. He's fine now.

I saw Mladen: he's in the HVO.*

Sometimes I go into the city centre (which means I still have a taste for adventure, ha, ha!) It really is interesting. There are posters all over the place telling people to 'Beware of snipers' wherever there's an intersection facing Mount Trebevic. The road the 'B. B.' disco's in is a case in point.

So when you go along one of these streets it's a case of on your marks, get set and run like the wind praying that the chap up there won't get you. What do you think about that? And when I get home people are going on and on about some grenade that's fallen in Tito Street, or in front of the big shops, and I start to ask myself where I was at that moment. It happens every time. That's how life is at present. But one lives and one hopes one will survive. The worst thing of all will be the winter. I don't even want to think about it. If hunger and disease don't kill us, the cold will.

I'm starting to run out of paper, so I shall move on to the greetings. Do listen to *Third World* by the Haustor. Pretend you're hearing it for the first time, without nostalgia. Nostalgia disturbs the mental processes; you would start remembering some good times, but bugger it . . . all! Listen to that album – especially 'The Gnomes in the Garden' track – and you will be here.

Another bit of news: Srecko is here, we see him every day.

Samir Causevic has been living in the Grbavica district for two months now, and all the phones are cut off. I don't even know if he's still alive. The most dreadful things have been going on there. I hope he's OK. I'm talking out of the top of my head, because where he is he can't be OK. But at least I hope he's still alive!

The animals in the zoo are dying of starvation. The tigress and the female panther died because their cages were too far away. Cretins! CNN showed a film about the zoo a few days ago (they won't let our reporters anywhere near). The propaganda machine of the 'Republika Serba' has stated that Izetbegovic's men feed Serbian children to the lions. I hope they die like those poor beasts they have left without food.

*HVO: Hrvatsko Vijece Odbrane. The Croatian Defence Council, the army of the Bosnian Croats.

Today is 31 July, and the city has come under tremendously heavy fire. I wonder what grenades the alarm sirens are warning me about. We are now being attacked, as they would say on the TV, 'with all the means at their disposal'. We've stopped going down to the cellar. Stuff the cellar. This is what life's all about! They've put all the phones out of action for fear of 'Fifth columnists'. I can't speak to the people in Dobrinja or Mojmilo any more, and not even to the people who live across the road.

Amar is with the Civil Protection people, dragging corpses out of the Miljacka river (side-splittingly funny).

I think about you. What are you up to?

Lada

Vienna, August 1992

To my friends in Belgrade,

I stuck it out for nearly four months. And now that I am here I am wondering how I did it.

Here is the order of events:

1. 'Be there at eight in the morning. A bus will come for you.' I did not even leave the cellar as the dawn was already stained with blood and defiled by the smoke of bombs.

    That was on May 2nd.

    On that morning Sarajevo ceased to be a city.

2. 'You can come to the airport. But you must be there before one o'clock.' I couldn't make it. No one was willing to risk his life in a car over those two murderous kilometres.

3. 'No civilian is allowed in the armoured car. There is one seat available in the minibus.' This I gave up to the painter Mersad Berber.

4. 'There are now seats available in three armoured cars.' And so I was able to leave with Mitterand's young minister, Bernard Kouchner.

Butmir airport has been transformed into a military base. We are swallowed up by the cavernous vastness of a Hercules that is disgorging food and medicines with its engines running non-stop.

We take off.

Throughout this whole period of a hundred and fifty-five days, one thought alone has been on my mind: 'I would rather die than be mutilated. If they shoot me, so be it.'

While I was on guard at the gate outside the house, a grenade came whistling by only three metres away from me . . . but it never exploded. Immediately afterwards, a bullet hit the wall behind my left ear. That morning a boy was badly injured in Rade Koncar square. Another lad, running to help the first, was shot dead. They were firing at us as though we were puppets at a fairground.

Even men driving ambulances to the hospital were killed. I saw two of them at a broken traffic light with their heads hanging out of the cab windows. Will they show this too on television? Our cameramen are heroic, and even foreigners are saying: 'This is much worse than Vietnam'.

At night I watched the fiery trails of the grenades as they screamed overhead on their way to destroy all the trams and buses of the public transport services. Then they hit the milk distribution centre, the maternity hospital and the 'Vijecnica', our great, beautiful library where a hundred thousand volumes were reduced to cinders. Then it was the turn of the bakery.

The city was gutted. The water supply dwindled and then vanished completely. We were totally without electricity, so mountains of frozen meat had to be thrown away and the first reserves of food had disappeared.

I was saved by half a kilo of pork fat. I had offered, since no one else wanted the job, to take over the management and provisioning of the condominium. Each flat had been allocated half a kilo of pork fat, but the muslims refused it and so did my next-door neighbour, a Serb, because he had heard that there was to be a distribution of oil in the area.

I was left with the fat and a piece of bread that I cut into small squares to make it last longer.

From the start we were without wine, spirits and cigarettes. My neighbour gave me a bottle of grappa and I drank it alone, in the dark, to the last drop, without getting drunk. The composer Esad Arnautalic who lives in the Dobrinja area near the airport and used to get through a hundred cigarettes a day, now 'smokes' tea-leaves. The teacher Muhamed Filipovic clubbed together with some friends while they still had funds and bought a calf. They paid for it with Deutschmarks, but then didn't know what to do as none of them was able to butcher it.

The mayor has called me and asked me to start writing articles for some of the newspapers. I am collected by a young kamikaze driver who belts flat out past burning vehicles and the spectral remains of bombed buildings. We cut across the park, where cars were never allowed in 'pre-war' days, at lightning speed.

Since the beginning of May not even a cat has set foot in Obala street. Grass has grown over the tram-lines. In that very street an exceedingly dear friend of mine from the Lycée, the architect Vesna Bugarski, was killed.

The very fine ten-storey building that housed the newspaper *Oslobodjenje* has been bombed and completely burnt out. But even before that happened, the morale of most of the journalists had crumbled.

Ibrahim Ljubovic, probably the best painter in Sarajevo, fled from his burning studio in tennis shoes, abandoning twenty or so pictures that he had refused for years to sell at any price.

The sculptor Alija Kucukalic was killed at his own front door. The actor Nermin Tulic has lost both legs.

A neighbour of mine, the painter Afan Ramic, calmly carries on painting. He explains that, being so short, he is a difficult target.

The sadness is worse than the hunger and the hate that is swamping us.

An old friend of mine waits for me at his door and says: 'My son, don't come again. It is too dangerous.'

All the shops and all the tobacconists were wrecked and looted in the first few days. Books and old newspapers left on the shelves have disappeared too now that winter is on the way. They come in useful for lighting fires. Even the owners of food shops and cafés, who made sacks of useless money, have now switched from the black market to a much more lucrative trade in firearms.

Siba Krvavac, who wrote the screenplay of *Walter defends Sarajevo*, died in his bed. The teacher Stojan Tomic is also dead. His son carried him to the cemetery all on his own. He dug the grave, was driven away by a hail of bullets, and returned later to fill it in. There is no more room to bury the dead even in the parks. They have now begun to use the Kosevo football ground.

And yet my city survives.

I am now in Vienna. The choreographer Slavko Pervan called me yesterday from Bol, on the island of Brac. He wants to send me a copy of the famous *Hair* that, as he says, he 'staged in Sarajevo with only five actors'.

Here in Vienna I still cannot bear to sit near a window. I find the silence, without the whine of mortars and the echo of explosions, unnerving.

Dzavid Husic

Sarajevo, 7 August 1992
19.15 hours

Hey, baby,

I've been 'out' again! I thought I was used to the situation, but apparently I'm not. I'm now in a really black mood . . . the blackest that ever was?

I'm sitting here in the home of my 'husband' in Borko, with Chetniks only five hundred metres away. He and Miro went to the command post for supper and I'm sitting here listening to *October 1864* and looking at the emptiness around me. I went into town today and I must admit it was hard for me. It's dreadful to live in fear (do you remember Camus' *The Plague*?)

Today I trod in fresh blood, blood that was still wet on the road. But God himself must have been looking after me, because I then ran into Amar and stopped and chatted with him for a few minutes, and exactly where I would have been if I hadn't stopped, a 'small' grenade exploded.

I am in a state of absolute terror today!

Mario and Miro have just walked in. They are both telling whoppers. Miro says to tell you that he has killed three Chetniks and so has Mario.

Now here's a nice little story that is actually true as well. Today, when Mario was on guard duty, a Chetnik came right up to the bend in the road and called out 'Long live the king!'

Really quaint.

Yours,
Lada

Sarajevo, 27 August 1992

Dear Delo,

I am sitting here with your mother. We've been talking about all
kinds of things. We know that you're fine over there, that you are
playing, swimming, eating, getting sunburnt . . . Here grenades are
falling all the time and bullets fly in all directions.

You won't believe this, but it's true.

They held an audition the other day for boys who could sing. I
went along and we each sang three songs. I sang *Take the standard
Vikic, Juka* and *Where hate is meat and drink*. They chose me as
the best singer from our street. And I went to rehearsals every day.
Then they said that the festival would be the next day. The festival
began. I sang sixth and your father was one of the judges. When
the lady presenter called out my name, I went onto the stage and
began to sing. While I was singing *Dragan Cicovic*, the pianist let
me down and I made a mistake, but I got to the end of the song.
Then they called me and told me I had come second. I got some
presents. So the festival ended very well. I went into town the other
day and had my ear pierced and got an earring in the shape of a
lily, which is our emblem.

Now here's something that will really make you sit up. A few
days ago I had an ORANGE!!

And after that there's nothing else to tell you apart from some
news of our classmates that I know will interest you. I have seen
Nedim. He's here, he was wounded in the leg, in the head and all
over his body. But he's fine now. Vlado is a 'Chetnik'. Belma has
gone to Alipasino. Samir is at the seaside.

Look after yourself, Delo, I'm fine, write to me and I'll write
to you.

Cheers,
Haris

AU REVOIR

Sarajevo, 31 August 1992

Our dear children,

Yesterday the electricity came back on, after exactly one month and a day.

You are probably wondering how we managed. I don't know. All I know is that Mia and I got out of bed last night, turned on a switch, and – marvel of marvels – the light came on and we then went from one room to another switching them all on!

There is still no water, however. Even in the city centre it has been off for eight days. There's only a little left in a few springs up in the hills. We're hoping that now the power is back the water will come back too, because they have said that the pumps will be re-started. I am sending this letter with one of those lucky people who can leave Sarajevo.

This morning your father told me to make as much use of the electricity as possible before it's cut off again. I really don't know what he means. Electricity is not water, I can't fill the bath-tub with it!

Maja came round yesterday, very happy because they got their power back, two days before we did, and now they don't have to light a fire on the balcony to cook their meals.

The days pass by. They pass so quickly that sometimes we don't even know what day of the week it is. And we've forgotten all about months. Which is just as well, because if we start to think about the coming winter, we are seized by yet another terrible anxiety: how are we going to heat the place?

Avdo has already 'booked' a stove, and our other neighbour, Mesud, has installed the old stove from his mother's house. We seem to be going back, in a strange way, to the days of our childhood.

When I asked Mesud what he was going to use for fuel in the old stove, he replied: 'I counted all the cupboards in the apartment; there are dozens of them and all made of good heavy oak. They will each last for two days at least.'

This is just one of those things that happen in wartime that at the start I found so hard to accept. Now I'm hardened.

When I got home on Monday after that call I managed

to put through to Kenan, I told Mia about it and she said, 'Dear God, what a lot we'll have to talk about when we meet again'.

And I thought, '*If* we meet again.'

My greatest wish is just to FORGET EVERYTHING as soon as possible, immediately this war ends.

Too many dreadful things have happened during these five months, things that we cannot and should not talk about, or they will be with us to the day we die.

All we can do for the present is to try to find the strength to survive until the nightmare is over.

We are none of us quite our normal selves. Mia is positively radiant this morning because the power is back and she hopes the water will be turned on soon, which means she will no longer have to fetch it in barrels.

We are all helping each other and being as supportive as possible.

Yesterday your father finished the book I was telling you about in my last letter. Now Mia and I have to type it up, but we are concerned about your father. What will he do now?

Mia puts a very brave face on everything. When she gets depressed we start talking about you, but we soon have to stop because that upsets us more than ever.

Even reminiscing about Milan, the little things we enjoyed there, the places we saw, is banned! All we think about is that we mustn't allow the present situation to get the better of us, and that one day we will once more see the sea at Makarska, which has become something of a symbol for us.

A symbol of peace, because there are no bombs there, a symbol of freedom because there you can walk out of the house knowing that you will return to it alive, and last of all, and only last, a symbol of food.

For Mia it also means sleeping again in her own bed, because she has had more than enough of sleeping in what Pervan dubbed the 'passage of freedom'.

Besides, this imprisonment within four walls makes so many things appear unreal. A friend of your father's was saying to him the other day, 'If I had fallen like you from the top of the tree in Sarajevo into this pit of hell, I should be beating my head against the wall five times every morning.'

We are not beating our heads against the wall. On the contrary, we are coping!

They have said that they will start to issue passports in September. We will try to get ours. How wonderful it would be if they opened up those famous 'corridors' and we could get in the car and drive to the coast! Or is that asking too much?

A few weeks ago I raced to the police station in Marijin Dvor to collect the new licence and number plates. It cheered us up because it meant a change. The new plates are SA-570312, and your father has even promised that this time he will learn the number by heart!!

Friends and relations are all alive and well. I even managed to get to the television centre today with Nebojsa.

Uncle Ahmo and Aunt Fata are well. You could never imagine them as they are now. Ahmo, always so elegant in the past, now carries barrels of water from Asikovac and says he finds it all 'so amusing'.

Vedad is not well but he doesn't want Selma, in Frankfurt, to know. They have discovered that he has gallstones, but with dozens of dying people arriving in the hospitals every day, that is a complaint for which no doctor has the time to spare.

And he — and I understand now why you love him so much — suffers so bravely. His brother Jasmin is in a dilemma, not knowing what to do with the children now that winter is approaching.

He is exploring the possibility of sending them to America. This would seem to be good common sense, but I personally don't agree with it. The parents, however, must do what they think right.

So many people collect in my editorial office that writing has become impossible. Still, it is only while I am there that I have any feeling of normal life.

We miss you all dreadfully, though perhaps I shouldn't say that!

There are so many things I should still like to ask, above all about our adored grandson.

Sanja, when the telephones are working properly again, you will be able to tell us a bit about him, and that will be wonderful!

CUVAJTE SE, take care of yourselves! As always, those words remind me of my little Zlatan running down the stairs and shouting back at me, 'I'll take care of myself, Granny!'

We love you all so much,
Nadja, Mia and Sefik

Sarajevo, 1 September 1992

Auntie's little darling,

Three long months have passed since we were last together, and I so much want this letter to bring you a little happiness. You are always in our thoughts and we are happy to know that you have settled down and are safe. I know how difficult it is for you, being so far away from us all, my darling Nincek, but time passes very quickly and every day brings the prospect of being together again one step closer. It is an enormous relief to me that you are well away from the horrors of this war which has been thrust on us against our will. We are all paying the price for political stupidity, but whenever you get depressed and homesick for your family and friends, just remember how lucky you are to be safe, able to study, to sleep soundly and to carry on a normal life. Thousands and thousands of boys and girls here in Sarajevo go to sleep with the boom of explosions in their ears, they have no time to play, and they smile less and less.

So when you feel sad, get together with your friends and try to cheer each other up, remembering that nothing bad can last for ever.

I'm glad you are going to school, and that you are learning foreign languages. Uncle Mirza is particularly pleased to hear that you are carrying on with your drawing and developing your artistic talent. When you come back you can teach us Italian, and Masa, Zenja and I will be your pupils.

Write and tell us about yourself, because that is what we want to hear most of all. Tell us what you do in your spare time, what you do at school, describe your impressions of the town where you are staying and the girls and boys you meet. Do you remember the little pet-names that Auntie had for you when you were tiny? She used to call you Auntie's precious, her little chickie-chickie-chatterbox. Now you are growing up fast and have probably already started to cast the odd glance at the boys. If you haven't remembered to do so before, you might start to keep a diary, recording your thoughts and anything that strikes you as important. If you rely solely on your memory, so many things may get forgotten. Now I will tell you about us. Your mother and father are well. They live like everyone else in Sarajevo, spending much of their time getting in food and firewood, because there's no electricity and very often no water either.

Grandpa comes round sometimes. He's well, but has got so thin . . .

Olja has grown into a fine young man and Zenja keeps getting taller. He's taller than I am now. They hardly ever go out because they have so few friends left in the neighbourhood. They spend most of their time reading books. Masa knits and tries to amuse the smaller children by reading poetry and stories to them. The schools are closed and we have to try by every means we can to make sense of life under these conditions. All the telephone cables are out of action and we have never been able to get through to you. Just once we did manage to get through to the institute where you are living, but while they were trying to find you the line went dead. You can imagine our grief. But we shall try again.

That's all, my darling Nina. We love you and think about you all the time. Auntie sends you a thousand kisses.

Aunt Jasna

Sarajevo, 1 September 1992

My darling little girl,

At last I've got the chance to write to you, although luckily, in spite of everything, I have managed to learn that you are well. It was Nuno who told me, having heard from Ajna in Milan. I always try to get messages to you in Rimini via the radio link. I'm writing this letter in a terrific hurry because I still have to prepare the radio news bulletin. It's half past two in the afternoon of 1 September and I'm in the nuclear shelter. A Spanish journalist has offered to take this letter to Ajna who will send it on to you.

I am well, but ever since you told me, on the telephone, not to venture away from the district too often, I have become exceedingly nervous. I have only been out of the house once, to try to reach you by satellite phone from the chairman's office, but the line was dead.

I am working as usual, doing both the day and night shifts, so I am seldom at home. Granny is well, and we often speak to each other on the phone. She is alone in her apartment. I spend a great deal of time with Kravic and Brajlovic and we talk about you very often. Old people and children are absolutely forbidden to go out into the streets. I drive to work, but you needn't worry because I use a 'secret route'. I think about you all the time, especially when I'm in the shelter. I know I did the right thing in sending you to Italy. I hope you will be able to phone from time to time. Belgrade has cut off all communication between us and the rest of the world. At this very moment they are fighting for the liberation of Sarajevo, and today is the crucial day. They have already managed to liberate several zones in the city, Nedjarici and Ilidza only partially, all the others completely.

We have been without water and electricity for a month now, but we're managing to survive. At Radio Sarajevo I get a packed lunch on a tray, so I subsist on that.

You mustn't worry, my darling, you have not been abandoned. I hope that you will be able to come back very soon, but you will be much better off in Italy for the winter, because here there is nothing to eat and no means of keeping warm.

In my last letter I enclosed a few lire that Boki had given me, and I will send you some more as soon as communications are restored.

Foreign journalists are travelling to and fro all the time and I will see if I can send something with one of them.

I am having to write this letter as fast as I can because I have to hand it over, so I can't say all I would like to. However, I wrote you another, six pages long, only yesterday. Be good, my love, take care of yourself and try to accept this new state of affairs. Everything will be very difficult here for quite a while at least. Having coped with your absence I can face anything. Sweetheart, you must never lose hope that things will be alright one day. I was so sorry that I couldn't dress you better when you went away, but I sincerely hope they will give you some clothes for the autumn. A delegation from The Children's Embassy, accompanied by Italian journalists, will be visiting you before long. They are going to do a documentary about you, which means we'll able to see you . . . I AM HAVING TO CONTINUE IN CAPITALS BECAUSE MY MACHINE HAS GOT STUCK AND REFUSES TO TYPE ANYTHING ELSE. THE SCHOOLS HERE ARE NOT GOING TO REOPEN SO I HOPE YOU WILL GO TO SCHOOL THERE AND THAT YOU WILL LEARN ITALIAN. DO KEEP UP YOUR ENGLISH, BECAUSE YOU WILL FIND IT VERY USEFUL. I AM GOING TO FIND OUT ABOUT SENDING YOU TO AMERICA. I'M TOLD IT SHOULD NOT BE DIFFICULT.

MY DARLING DON'T BLAME ME BECAUSE MY LET-TER IS SO MESSY. I'VE HAD TO WRITE IT IN STAGES.

I AM STUDYING ITALIAN, I MANAGED TO GET HOLD OF A BOOK AND A CASSETTE, SO WHEN WE NEXT SEE EACH OTHER WE CAN SPEAK IN ITALIAN. MY PRECIOUS I MUST CLOSE NOW BECAUSE I HAVE TO HAND MY LETTER OVER.

I LOVE YOU HEAPS AND HEAPS AND AM DYING TO SEE YOU AGAIN.

LOTS OF HUGS
MAMMA
XXX

P.S. GIVE MY REGARDS TO SIGNORA ADELA AND TELL HER THAT I SAW HER HUSBAND ACO AND THAT HE IS WELL.

Sarajevo, 4 September 1992

My dear Ivana and Mirza,

I can't believe it, but your handwriting, your own beautiful handwriting, is here in my hands at this very moment! I have read your letter a thousand times at least. To touch something so fresh, smelling of the warm sea, is a privilege very few people in Sarajevo can enjoy in the present circumstances.

I am trying to picture the two of you, 'Ivana, the mother, with her beautiful and lovable little boy who has conquered all hearts on the island'. I am quoting your husband's words. The description is so lovely, and becomes more so every day because I renew it in my mind's eye. The only photo I have of Mirzo shows him as a little 'frog' in the red plastic baby bath. And now he's a little boy in the blue sea!

I can understand perfectly well the fear and horror you feel when you see the pictures on television, because it is truly horrible here, as if hell itself had suddenly opened beneath our feet.

I often wonder where the men here find their strength, their will to carry on and to preserve their common sense.

This is something unreal, incredible!

To talk about common sense is very difficult, given that the criteria that prevail today are so very different from what they used to be.

My dear Vanjo, the fact that the two of you have managed to get away from here is worth everything to me. My wish is that nothing, not even a single person, nor a word, should come near you to upset the even tenor of your lives.

If you make yourself 'think positive' that is how it will be!

Dragan is well and my family is all in good health and one piece, as are our friends Vesna, Alma and Sonja. We phone each other from time to time. Alma and I often manage to meet.

I love you so very much!

I wish you a happy 1 October, 14 November and New Year.

Yours, Asja

P. S. Neven and Sanja have a daughter.

Sarajevo, 12 September 1992

My darling Ivana,

Your latest message, like all the other news of you and our little one, has made me so happy (if happiness is a word one can still use at this time in Sarajevo) that I can't describe what I feel. I didn't know, I didn't realize that I could love you both so much, and that without you nothing is worth bothering about! Everything else is meaningless . . . I live and fight only for you.

I actually made it to Dobrinja* and had a look at our apartment. It hasn't been hit by grenade-fire but only anti-aircraft guns and could have been a lot worse. Our neighbour Fikret has been keeping an eye on it and doing a bit of tidying up. I only brought one thing away with me from the apartment, the album with all the photographs of the two of you. I never stop looking at it, and think of you all the time!

Don't worry too much about me, I am very careful. I see your brother Zarko from time to time. He's stationed in one of the faculty buildings, and is a member of the light anti-aircraft artillery brigade, so he doesn't have to go and fight. Don't worry, he's not in any danger because they only have to be prepared to act in case of an aerial attack.

Once we're together again, nothing will ever separate us.

I love you, I love you, I love you

Zlatan

---

*Dobrinja: An outlying suburb of Sarajevo, one of the worst-affected parts of the city and virtually inaccessible for much of the time.

Sarajevo, 15 September 1992

My dear brother,

I know you will be surprised to get this letter. I have tried to write
to you so many times! Now, quite by chance, I have discovered
that Caritas and UNPROFOR are prepared to carry letters, so I
am sending this in the hope that you will get it.

We are all well at the moment.

The situation here is terrible but we trust that we can cope and
that we shall survive. There's not much to eat and fruit and
green vegetables were completely unobtainable even throughout
the summer.

Now autumn is in the air and I don't know how we will cope
with the cold weather without any glass in the windows. The
grenades shattered it all and there's no hope of replacing it. We
can only hope that the war will end and that everything will get
back to normal. Take care of yourself.

Your sister Seka

[Enclosure]

Dear Cousin Jasmin,

Mother is making a rice cake today. She is also making rissoles.
We have discovered so many recipes and when, God willing, this
is all over, we will send you a stack of them.

Did you know it is possible to make cakes without eggs and
butter? You ought to see what we have managed to do with
Eurocrem and humanitarian aid!

So don't worry about us. I think about you a lot.

Your cousin Zehra

Sarajevo, 17 September 1992

My darling children,

The first thing I want to tell you is that mummy loves you very, very much and thinks about you every day and every minute of the day . . .

Omar, I beg you to be patient until this war is over. You undoubtedly see reports from Sarajevo on the television and may know what the situation is like. It is dreadful for the children here. The city is shelled every day and the children spend nearly all their time in cellars or shut up in their apartments. Try to imagine what it's like when the sun is shining outside and you're not allowed out of the cellar . . . The schools are all closed and many children have left the city just as you did. I believe that all your classmates and the mistress too have now fled from Sarajevo.

But you will return to your city of Sarajevo when all this is over, as it surely will be sooner or later! But we must be patient.

Your school is closed, and is now occupied by soldiers. Once the war is over it will be a school once more.

Many buildings in Sarajevo have been wrecked and reduced to rubble, but we shall rebuild everything eventually.

I am telling you all this so that you can understand that Havar is much better off with Granny and his little brother. You can swim, you can play in the fresh air all day long, and you might even be going to school!

If you go to school, don't worry about your marks. Even if you get twos and threes and fives, no one will be cross with you! Learn what you think you need to learn. At the moment, in the war, the most important thing is to stay alive, and there will be plenty of time later on to catch up with your education.

With God's help, I shall send you to an English boarding school when you are old enough. Ask Granny to explain what that means.

I am very proud of my two handsome, intelligent sons, and of you especially, because I know you are a great help and support to your grandmother. You can and you must help her, you must look after little Sanjin, run errands for her, keep your things tidy, and wash yourself. You must help Ivana with baby Mirza. You're ten years old now and big enough to do these things.

Now I must tell you about my life. Papa and Granny Mulija stayed in our apartment in Dobrinja. Don't worry about Papa, he's well and so is Granny. Grandpa, Uncle Edi, Koja and I now live in a flat near Granny's office. We are no longer allowed into Grbavica, but I hope that we will soon be able to return home.

I go to work every day, and this is why I could not come with you. The war makes everyone suffer one way or another. Some have lost their homes, some have been wounded, some arrested, and some separated from their loved ones like us. It is hard for you, and for us too, but there are many people who have suffered much more. We are all alive and healthy, thank God, and this is what matters most.

No one can enter or leave the city, it is completely surrounded. As soon as there is a way out, Grandpa, Hana, Orhan and Vedran will come to join you. When mummy can leave her work, she will come to see you too. I cannot say when this is likely to be. For the moment we must all be patient and try to survive, so that when the war is over we can return to a normal life.

Knowing that you are safe is an enormous relief. It is very difficult even to find food here; it is always scarce and the only things available are rice and pasta. No fruit, vegetables, milk, eggs or butter. The adults manage to put up with this reasonably well, but it's much harder for the children. People will try to get all their children away, if they possibly can, before winter sets in.

Granny tells me that you have written me a letter, but I haven't received it yet. I should very much like you to keep a diary or something of that kind, so that I can read it later. I want so much to know how you feel, what you think about, what you are doing all this time when I am not with you. Write it all down in a notebook so that you won't lose it, and we'll read it together next time I see you. I should also love to hear about little Sanjin, to know if he has grown, what words he can say now, if you two get on well together, and if you do what Granny tells you.

For the moment Granny is EVERYTHING to you both, and you must be good and obedient. I suspect that she worries a great deal about us and that she finds looking after Sanjin very tiring. You must help her.

Now I want to ask you to do something for me. When you wake up every morning, give one kiss to Sanjin and one to Granny, and tell them, 'This is from Mamma Aida'. That's not too difficult, and it would mean so much to me.

And please, I beg you, speak to Sanjin about his mummy and don't let him forget me. You are a big boy and I know that you won't forget me, but he is so little and I am so frightened that he may not remember me. Talk to him about our home, your toys, the walks we used to have, the games we played, about everything that existed before the war, and all that we shall do together afterwards.

Your Mummy who loves you so very much – UP TO THE SKY!!!!!!!!

Autumn 1992

In my dream I wander through the rubble
in the old part of the city
looking for a piece of stale bread
my mother and I inhale the fumes
of gunpowder
and pretend that it is the aroma
of cake and kebabs.
We hurry although it is nine o'clock at night
and we may be hurrying towards the grenade 'with our
  number on it'
then an explosion roars through the street of dignity*
many people are wounded
sisters, brothers, mothers and fathers.
I reach out and touch a wounded hand
I touch death.
Terrified I realize that this is not a dream
but only another day in Sarajevo.

Edina, aged 12
Sarajevo, November 1992

*Vase Miskin street was known locally as the 'Street of Dignity' until it became
the scene of the Bread Queue Massacre, after which it was referred to as the
'Street of Affront'.

23 September
General Philippe Morillon, second in command of the United Nations Protection Forces in the former Yugoslavia, is appointed head of the forces in Bosnia-Hercegovina.

30 September
General Philippe Morillon arrives in Sarajevo. The UN General Secretary, Dr Boutros-Ghali, asks the Security Council to sanction a four or five fold increase in the number of UN troops in Bosnia-Hercegovina to provide escorts for the convoys carrying humanitarian aid to Sarajevo and other besieged cities.

October
The first clashes between Croat forces and the Bosnian army.

31 October
The international community proposes the setting up of an 'International War Crimes Tribunal' in the former Yugoslavia.

November
Unicef announces that from the start of the war in Bosnia-Hercegovina until 10 November the number of people killed was 128,126, of whom 12,818 were children. Of the 132,170 people wounded, 33,042 were children.

4 November
The last surviving animal in the Sarajevo Zoo, a brown bear, dies of starvation.

Sarajevo, October 1992

Darling,

Two months have now passed since we last saw you, and we don't expect to see you for another four or even longer. But try not to be sad. It's better for you, and for us, that you are far away. We know that you are well, that you have some good friends, that you are learning Italian and going to school. We also know that you have good food to eat and that you have been given some clothes. Here in Sarajevo you would have had none of this. The situation is difficult, there is a lot of firing, grenades are falling everywhere, but we are all well.

Some people are no longer with us. Ahmo, Aunt Esma's son, was killed, and Vedad and Mirza have both been wounded. They're in hospital, but recovering. Vanja was killed by a grenade, and Aunt Fata and Uncle Mirko are distraught. Even little Amela, the granddaughter of Avdo Islamovic who lives in our block, is no more. And Selma, Edina's cousin, has also been killed. We are still in Alipasino Polje and we are reasonably comfortable here. Our diet is always the same, of course: macaroni and rice and, very occasionally, some beans. Your mother has become a proper little housewife and is always inventing new recipes with rice. Papa goes to work every day and always brings us something back. We have had no power for over a month. Papa bakes the bread at work, but we are in the dark from five o'clock in the evening, and this is really dreadful. We have had no water supply for ten days and have to queue for two or three hours every day to get any at all. Mamma does all the cooking in the communal kitchen on the eighth floor. We've fixed up a little stove on the balcony to keep us warm in the winter if there is no electricity. So now we're collecting firewood. In Sarajevo, chopping wood has become something of a national sport. As I was saying, Mamma spends most of the day cooking, Papa has his work, and so the days pass. Grandfather gets frustrated, having nothing to do but lie and read all day long. I go and see friends in the evening, but in the daytime I get bored at home. However, we play cards and somehow manage to kill the time.

We often go to see Aunt Alma and Uncle Enver. Vanja and Sasa never go out, they're bored too. A grenade fell right on top of their car and completely destroyed it.

We often visit Bahra and Momo, and they always ask after you.

Papa keeps in contact with other members of the family by phoning them from work because our phone is dead. The only phones that are working are those in the city, so calling you would be out of the question.

Ermin escaped from Grbavica a month ago and has told us about the situation there. Our apartment has been taken over by Chetniks. A grenade fell on our car too and that is no more. No one is allowed to enter Grbavica and all our stuff is still there. I am most upset about the photographs and videos. Everything else can be replaced eventually.

I don't know if there's any way you can get a letter to us. If you can, don't be lazy but write. What are you doing? What are your friends like? How are you? Have you learnt to speak Italian? Have you got an Italian boyfriend? Don't forget the 'All Star' tennis shoes size 44 (that was a joke) and do write to us!

Give our love to all our friends, especially Vedrana and Nevena and Auntie Lila. Be good, learn all you can, and when you come back after this damnable war you can tell us all about it in peace and quiet.

With love and kisses from
Papa Zoran, Grandpa Nijaz,
Mamma Emira and your brother Orhan

As you see, we each signed individually to let you know beyond any doubt that we are all still alive.

Sarajevo, 10 October 1992

Dear Teacher,

I had a visit today from a lady and two gentlemen working for Unicef. They came to see what my living conditions were like. They asked me all kinds of questions, and also if I wanted to write a letter and if so to whom. I said I would like to write to my teacher, so they told me to write the letter and they would deliver it.

How are you? How is your family? I am well, and so are my parents and grandparents.

We have just come up from the cellar because a grenade has fallen very close to the building. When we're in the cellar I study, write, do maths exercises and read. I have taught myself to write the Latin script, too. I can't wait for this hateful war to end so that I can return to the school I love and see you and all my dear dear friends.

Papa told me that he saw you one day and I was very sad and cried because you have not been to see us. If you ever find yourself anywhere near here, please come in.

With much love,
Aida

My parents send their kindest regards.

Sarajevo, 10 October 1992

My dear sister,

There has been enormous excitement in the house since yesterday when your food parcel arrived from France. We were all too excited to sleep, and could think of nothing else. We haven't seen so much food since the start of the war. We will try to eke it out and make it last all winter. We think about you always and about how wonderful it would be if we were all together somewhere warm.

From time to time we see pictures on the television of the sleek, well-fed people in other parts of the world, and it seems so absurd that they should sit there, not giving a damn about the fact that here in Bosnia we are dying like flies.

But don't worry, somehow our nation will manage. By dint of not eating we have become lighter on our feet – everyone has shed between 15 and 20 kilos – so we can dodge the bullets and the bombs better than before.

We live an hour at a time, trying to survive all difficulties, waiting in vain for the skies to clear and the birds to fly again. Then we shall be able to get out again, go for a walk down the road, meet our friends. We have a certain pride, a certain sense of achievement in having adapted to this subhuman life-style, and perhaps it is this that gives us the strength to carry on. We can cope even if our city is crumbling around us and its hospitals are filled with the dying and mutilated bodies of our young people.

I hope this war ends, that the world will realize that it is completely mad and that it must not continue.

Winter is about to set in. Luckily it is later than usual and the weather is still mild.

You'll see, something will happen before winter comes. We have suffered enough.

With much love,
your sister Seka

Sarajevo, 10 October 1992

Darling,

Every time I sit down to write to you, I want to scream. I write
without knowing if you have received any of my letters.

Today is Sunday. It's raining, it's bitterly cold and for a month
we have had no water and no light. The Kravic family is in a state of
great agitation and anxiety because they have been told they might
be able to leave tomorrow. This is by no means certain, however,
as when you were about to leave with UNPROFOR.

If they go, Neda will ring you as soon as they reach Abazia. She
may even come to see you.

We, the parents of children being looked after by the authorities
in Milan, are always in touch. And we often speak about you.

We have been wondering why your escort Adela has never
phoned. Could you please ask her to do so as soon as possible.

A colleague on the paper *Slobodna Dalmacjia* sent me a tran-
script of your interview with an Italian journalist in Djelo. Nuno
Arnautalic and I wept as we read it.

A journalist who came to see me said he may be able to arrange
for me to speak to you by satellite. It's very expensive, so when I
call you, speak at once and tell me how you are getting on
in Italy.

Within Sarajevo the phones are working again, so I hear from
my friends. A few days ago I heard from Biza that his sister Raza
had been killed.

Ajla is also waiting to leave Sarajevo, but so far has been unable
to find a place in the convoy. It's very difficult, and you don't know
how lucky you were to get out.

People are now desperate to send at least their youngest children
away, because our worst enemies, cold and hunger, are about to
strike.

I manage what with one thing and another, and everything is
easier for me knowing that you are being properly fed.

Goran is recovering, but will never be the same again.

Desa hasn't received the parcel even though the arrangements
seemed to be functioning well. She spends all her time at the
hospital because she prepares Goran's food (there's none at the
hospital), so she often sleeps there. She has knitted you a cardigan

and asked my advice about what kind of buttons to put on it. I didn't know whether to laugh or cry.

I see you in my dreams, all blurred, and wake up in tears. I miss you terribly, and am doing all I can to get out of Sarajevo. I beg you to continue learning English as well as Italian, as you must realize now how important foreign languages are in today's world. Schools are nonexistent here; the children stay at home and cannot go out because the firing is heavier than ever.

Although I've lost 10 kilos I'm tubby compared to most.

But one day all this will be over.

Meanwhile, you must be a good girl and think hard about everything you do. Don't let the discipline worry you, but try to learn something from every new experience. Be, as you said in the interview, strong like all children in such a situation have to be. You're my wise little woman.

I hope you managed to make contact with your father, and if you speak to him tell him that I shall expect to hear all about you next time.

Tell him that he must ring his mother, too, and send her a parcel by the Red Cross. With my salary I can buy three packets of cigarettes a month, while other people can only buy one. My pension hasn't been paid in for several months.

Do make friends with the other children, and don't grumble if things go wrong from time to time. It made me dreadfully sad when I heard you say on the phone 'You can't imagine what it's like here.' I know it's not easy for you, alone as you are, but maybe you have forgotten what life is like here. Be sensible and remember that the most important thing is life itself.

I love you very much and can't wait to see you again.

Your mamma

Sarajevo, 12 October 1992

Dear Jasmin,

They have told us that at long last they may be able to get a letter to you. We have already written dozens but have never had a reply.

We heard news from Papa yesterday. He told us that he's confident that he can escape from Banja Luka and that he will come to you in Rovinj.

We shall be much happier knowing that you are together.

We wanted to let you know that we are all, for the moment, still fine. We also wanted to ask if you could send us a food parcel, because the situation here is deteriorating all the time and we don't know how we are going to manage.

We've got no water, no power, no gas now.

We go down to the street door and make a fire with the little wood that we have, like gipsies.

But you mustn't worry about us. This war will come to an end and everything will be better.

Much love from all of us,

Seka, Jasna, Sanja, Maja and Anka

Sarajevo, 12 October 1992

My darling,

There's just a tiny, perhaps infinitesimal possibility that this letter will find its way to you. If it does, you will know that I am still alive, that I love you, that I think of you always and miss you terribly. If it doesn't, I shall try again and again until I either succeed or snuff it. And the latter is no figure of speech seeing that dozens of innocent people are dying in the city.

I now realize how difficult it is to write this letter. I don't want to paint too graphic a picture of this hell that is Sarajevo now, of darkness, hunger, thirst, fear. As I write – it's just after six o'clock in the evening – large-calibre grenades are coming over the house; they are destroying Ciglane. Sarajevo is in a terrible state of devastation. A grenade fell on the roof of the restaurant you designed in Bascarsija and the façade was damaged by shrapnel. One day, when this madness is over, you will have a lot to do.

You know, I can honestly say that I communicate with you continuously, and I feel as if we have already agreed about the plans for our house by the lake. You will produce the designs, of course, and I shall instruct you about certain details. I have several ideas (inspired by the war).

Oh . . . Oh. Right at that moment a large-calibre grenade fell in Nemanjina street. They are probably aiming at the school, now used as a barracks. Everything is shaking, especially around here.

It occurs to me now and then what a good idea it was for you to take the children away . . .

I had to break off for a moment because just at that moment a big grenade landed right in front of the Libyan embassy in K. Petrovica street. And then another, tearing off part of the embassy roof. This is the worst attack we've had. If one of those grenades fell on this place, it would blow it into a million smithereens. Everything I've described has happened during the last twenty minutes.

. . . It's morning now. The darkness (we have no electricity) made it impossible to finish my letter. As I finish it now, the courtyard at No. 5 Takovska street is blazing furiously in the wake of incendiary bombs.

The situation is changing from one moment to the next.

In closing, my darling, I beg you to take care of yourself and not to forget that I love you so much that it hurts.

Pavle*

*Further letters from Pavle to his wife appear on pages 77, 82, 85, 87, 114, 117, 127, 161, 166–9, 170, 171.

Sarajevo, 14 October 1992
12 o'clock, a sunny day

My dear daughters, my darling kittens,

Before I say anything else I must tell you that I miss you terribly, and I am happy that the two of you are together. I am sure, too, that the situation will improve. Your mother has already written to you to tell you what we think:
  1. about the PARCEL you want to send. There's no point, because everything gets stolen in the post.
  2. about the POODLE you were thinking of buying in Italy. There's no point, because Bessy is about to have puppies!!
  I should like to give you a brief description about the situation here, that is since you, Boki, left. Between April and September it deteriorated drastically, and when you read these few lines of mine you will understand how much better off you are where you are.
  Mummy and I go to bed at eight every evening, and since there's no electricity we have to sleep willy nilly. There's no light, no TV, no radio, no record-player. The power's been off for thirty days now. We try to make do with oil lamps, incidentally very expensive. We cover ourselves up with three blankets apiece and lie there, like idiots, with our eyes shut.
  And then, having gone to bed at eight, we get up at six in the morning. I get dressed at once, as if I were going out, and return to bed for an hour, fully dressed. Then I get up again, in the dark, because it's wet and cold outside, and go to the bathroom where there's no water, and just dab my eyes.
  I only shave twice a week. The water is terribly cold – we can't heat it without electricity – and none too clean, being rainwater. Having got completely frozen while 'washing' myself in this way, I have to spend a penny and tuppence but there's no toilet paper and thus occupied, in the dark, I feel like crying. Given these conditions, thank heaven we haven't caught influenza or anything like that! Afterwards I go to the kitchen and drink a cup of ice-cold tea and then set out for the long walk down to what used to be the 'Trebevic' cable railway station to collect 25 litres of water. On my way I pass the market where all you find now is old shirts, old shoes, lighters and a kind of plum jam. And, of course, you can buy nothing without German marks!

And then there's the queue for bread and one never knows if there is going to be any or not. The bread queue is 50–70 metres long, while the queue for water can be as much as 100 metres, and it frequently comes under fire.

Anyway, we cope with this too, and I get back home at about ten where Mummy has already made coffee on the gas ring which we can still use because we still, luckily, have some gas, but it won't last long, and heaven knows what we shall do then. The hour or so we spend drinking coffee is the nicest time of the day, because we talk about you and about how happy we are that you are not here and being subjected to all this misery. And we feel that even if you are far away you are still a part of us.

The few litres of water I collected must be made to last several days. And now, already tired, I go out to chop some firewood. I have already cut down nearly all the trees round the building; we use the wood for cooking lunch and supper. Rizo and the Jokic boys chop wood with me and we have to defend it from those cunning rascals who would like to help themselves without working for it.

We have rebuilt the old wood-burning stove, now used by all the tenants in the condominium. We've set it up in Jasar's garage which has become the warmest place to be, and we go and warm ourselves there provided it is not raining. We collect bits of wood from all over the city to take home. While dinner's being prepared I go out again, but Boki dear, I haven't tried to find any eggs since you left. Anyway, there aren't any.

We usually eat between twelve and one, and then we tog ourselves up as if we were off for a mountain hike, because by three it is already dark and getting colder. Your friends come to see us and ask if we need any help, but for Mummy and me it's enough to know that you two are not here.

The telephone is also out of action and we cannot speak to anyone even within Sarajevo. After lunch Mummy and I have a cigarette and smoke until two o'clock when it starts to get dark. That darkness with no warmth, no music, no TV.

Every day is the same, cold, dark and surrounded by filth. But we can hold out for a long time. The important thing is that you are safe, because if you were here and I couldn't provide you with the essentials of life, I should have died a long time ago. While the situation in Sarajevo persists we have to put our emotions into the deep-freeze. That is the only way we can manage to live and to survive. When we are together again we can 'coddle' each other as we used to.

But you are now grown up, you are twenty-five and must understand that this is life. We have to accept the inevitable, we have no alternative. It is not our fault, but a stroke of fate. You, Boki, were always afraid this would happen. When all's said and done, my kittens, what is happening is precisely what we feared back in May. The only thing we didn't foresee is that we wouldn't be able to see you any more.

But this too will pass.

Don't worry about us. We're well and happy to know that you are together and far from here, because at your age and with your tastes – for music, television, telephones, warmth, water, coffee, bars, young men – you would have been miserable here without a doubt.

Our only loves, you mustn't be without money. Get some from B. because he owes me!

Now I must BREAK OFF, but not FINISH.

We love you very, very, very much.

We kiss you and hope to see you soon. I don't know when it will be, only that it will be by the sea, in Italy.

Papa, Mamma and Bessy*

P.S. Don't let the thought of birthdays make you sad. All that matters is to think of each other on such days, and then they will be wonderful.

*The winter is Nikola Nesovic. See also letters on pp. 143 and 147 and the note on p. 172.

Sarajevo, 16 October 1992

My darling,

It's now three months since we saw you and we miss you terribly, though the thought that you are safe makes us feel better.

I can tell you at once that we are well, or as well as one can be in Sarajevo at this time. I only mean that we are alive and in good health. Unhappily, Tina Pekmez and Kemo Selimovic are both dead, and that makes us tremendously sad, but life goes on. Now I'll tell you what each of us does, beginning with Grandfather because he is the oldest. For him it is very difficult. He wanders around the house, reads his books and keeps himself to himself as usual. At home he wears two sweaters, a jacket and three pairs of socks because it is freezing.

Papa spends all day every day with the battalion and when he comes home he is tired and irritable and takes it out on us. But we are lucky to see him for only an hour or two each day. Don't worry about him: he does not have to go out and fight. He is in the engineering corps and his job is to rebuild bridges, repair railway tracks and roads, etc.

Mamma has developed a variety of skills. She has learnt to chop wood, knit, carry water, light the fire and cook. Zumra Bostandjic came to see us a few days ago. He told us about the current situation in Grbavica and said that a Chetnik called Obrad Golijanin is living in our apartment. He said we weren't to worry because he has promised not to take any of our stuff.

I don't know what else to write. We miss you dreadfully.

Lots of kisses,
your grandfather, father, mother and brother

Sarajevo, 16 October 1992

Dear Kenan, Zlatan and Sanja,

How are we? It's a beautiful day today because the electricity has come back, so despite the terrible times we live in, the flat is a wee bit livelier. When we had everything we didn't notice it: it seemed only normal to have power and water supplies. Now that we have nothing and that so much has been taken away, as soon as they dole out something with a medicine-dropper, we're happy. Calvary without the hill! Can you imagine the joy of being able to have a bath in a bathtub after weeks on end? And being able to cook a meal in the kitchen? And even a meal that is totally lacking in variety seems tasty provided it is hot and cooked in one's own kitchen.

My dears, so many things in our lives have changed suddenly and unexpectedly, and it will take a long time to get back to normal life. There are sounds, for example, that will always send a shiver down our spines because they are like the scream of a grenade, which is the ugliest sound in the world. And electricity. I can't imagine what it will be like to switch on the lights when darkness falls. And a heated room? Where food's concerned, we have discovered that we are not too greedy. Some things we have not tasted for months, but we don't miss them. It would, however, be nice if food had some taste to it. One's hair stands on end at the thought of sitting down and facing a bowl of the same old 'naked' pasta or rice yet again. Today is a feast-day, because humanitarian aid has allocated half a kilo of potatoes per person. It sounds frightful, but it is not. What is frightful is to realize how human beings can get used to anything. In the buildings nearby, birds were nesting in the holes made by the grenades! Life goes on.

I miss you all dreadfully. I want to speak to you, hear your voices, know whether you think about us as we think about you. It would be so lovely to see you all soon; to be with you in a normal world; to return to the world of the living; not to hear sounds that strike fear to one's heart; to be free to look out of the window; to be able to go out for a walk even on one's own. We miss you all.

Nadja

Sarajevo, 19 October 1992

Dear heart,

This will be the fifth time that I have tried to contact you. In three days' time it will be the 21st. Until now I have celebrated the day by listening to Bebek and lighting the candle in the evening. Now there is no power, no water, no nothing (to put it simply) apart from the chaos outside me and the sadness inside. One tries to organize one's life in such a situation and tries, albeit to a very limited extent, to make it more bearable, but everything is reduced to the level of survival.

Sarajevo is the largest concentration camp in the world. Months without light, water, food . . . in every way. As you know, I have never had any special reserves of foodstuffs. Forget variety! On average, I lose one kilo a week. I don't notice this myself, but the scales do. Yesterday they set fire to the gas supply lines and the bakery, so now we can't even get bread. Anyway, for a month now they've only been supplying hospitals and the military.

I have retrieved an old stove from the attic and collected everything that will burn, such as rags, bits of old furniture and cardboard boxes to light the fire and stop my teeth chattering, because winter is nearly here. I should be working outside the city, but because of all the bureaucracy at the Ministry for Foreign Affairs I have not, as you see, been able to get permission; however, I have not given up hope.

My one love, I can't tell you how much I want you and how much I miss you, and although in one way I am happy that you are safely away from here, in another way I think it would have been much easier to face these horrors together. I realize how selfish this is, but loneliness is a poison that corrodes the heart.

All my thoughts are with you. It's so painful to look in the wardrobe and stroke your clothes on which the loved scent is already becoming fainter, to glance at your photograph smiling down at me over the bed, to see the mules in the dressing room that have waited so long for you to slip into them, in short, you are everywhere, and yet so far away and out of reach.

I fear this time of separation, I am afraid that nothing will ever be the same again. Believe me, if the devil fetches me away, I shall go with you in my heart.

Today the weather is autumnal, with a warm wind blowing from the south that is melancholy, cruel, and I am weary.

I embrace you, my darling, and I kiss you!

Pavle

Sarajevo, 21 October 1992

Dear Sir,

This is the first time since the war began that I have had the opportunity of sending you any news about myself. We are still alive, but do not know for how long. My greatest regret is that I was unable to save my daughter from this hell. I imagine that you must have heard in Paris about the situation here. Sarajevo is a concentration camp. There is no water, no electricity, nothing to buy. What little food there is costs a fortune in Deutschmarks. I have not worked since the war started and our stocks are completely exhausted. Humanitarian aid supplies are distributed to us but they are scarce and insufficient to feed us, consisting as they do of half a kilo of flour or rice, occasionally half a kilo of sugar, quarter of a litre of oil, a tin of fish. We cannot even buy bread any longer. I have lost 17 kilos and Dragana is unrecognizable. This is why I have summoned up my courage and taken the liberty of writing to ask you to send us, if possible, a food-parcel. An Italian journalist who is leaving Sarajevo tomorrow is taking this letter with him and has promised to post it to Paris from Italy. Perhaps, with the help of UNPROFOR or UNHCR or the 'Equilibre' organization, it would be possible for you to find someone coming to Sarajevo who would be willing to bring a parcel.

My dear sir, I am sorry to write to you only to ask, but unfortunately fate has made everyone presently in Sarajevo a beggar, since without charity we could not survive.

I thank you, however, for all that you may be able to do or not do for us.

Yours respectfully,
Amir Hezirovic

Sarajevo, 25 October 1992

Dear Papa and everyone,

I have already written six times and have had only one reply from
you. We are very worried about you, Papa, because we know the
state you were in when you left for Banja Luka for your sister's
funeral.

Have you got any food? Have you got any clothes?

Here the situation is dreadful and we are all hoping for better
times. As far as food is concerned, we're all right for the moment
as we have received a parcel.

Everything here is exceedingly expensive. Half a kilo of macaroni
costs 2000 dinars, which is a month's salary for me.

Your pension arrived at the post office three months ago, but I
haven't been able to collect it yet because firing in the streets has
been so heavy and I am afraid to leave the house. I shall see if they
will send it to the bank.

But you needn't worry about it, as all the shops have gone
anyway, and there's nothing to buy.

Get a message to us somehow, I beg of you. Perhaps Caritas or
UNPROFOR could help.

Take care.

Mamma and Seka

Sarajevo, 28 October 1992

Dear Vanja!

The 'trains' are departing – as it were. Asja, Sonja and I are staying here. A friend of mine is leaving any day now with his family en route to Slovenia, and he will take my letter with him. I have exactly five minutes to write to you.

It is indescribably awful here. The meaning of life has been reduced to eating, washing and sleeping . . . and at least two out of these three things are sometimes beyond us. Asja and I very often see your husband. He's well, he's as handsome as ever, but feels lost without you. A few days ago he went to see Asja and said he couldn't remember your face. Asja reacted very swiftly and dug up one of your photos from somewhere and showed it to him.

Your brother, on the other hand, we haven't seen for a long time, but Zlatan told us that he was well. Asja and I are always together and sometimes we even manage to laugh. We try to joke about what is happening to us!

Last summer we did a bit of sunbathing outside the front door while grenades whistled over our heads just to keep us amused.

We've been trying to keep ourselves busy with some humanitarian work, by feeding the abandoned and starving animals. One young man who walked past said: 'It would be better if you were helping children'. We have spoken to Kaca and Vera. They are fine, which means they are still in one piece, their heads still on their shoulders.

A few days ago Asja and I went into town and I said to her jokingly: 'I've left my identity card behind. If I'm blown to bits you'll have to identify me!' Black humour is essential to survival.

Sonja is still in Otokar. Sanja, her brother Neven's wife, has had a baby. It's very difficult for them, having nothing to eat. Luckily she has her milk and can feed the baby, so that problem is solved for the time being. Sonja is depressed, but as always she has found an outlet in work. She has crocheted twenty pairs of gloves. They are wonderful, and she would like to sell them to those who still have the money for such things.

My Milan is at Kiseljak, working very hard, but there's absolutely no way that we can go and visit him. Vesna is working for UNPROFOR, but for the last month we haven't even been able to speak to her on the phone. I think she's well. Actually, Asja, who has seen Sonja only once since the beginning of the war, met her again a week ago. This is a real concentration camp.

Asja tells me that you have written to her and that you are both well. You were lucky to get away in time. Olja and little Ena couldn't get out until the end of August, and had a dreadful time! Every time a grenade landed the little one shouted 'Boom!' So sad . . . Now they are both with Malik in Malesia and we believe that they are fine, or at least one may hope so as we have had no news.

The present situation has 'uncovered' a lot of weak characters, but also many honest, good people. My only aim in life is to survive. I want nothing more . . .

I hope very much to see you in the near future.

With love,
Alma

P.S. A great big kiss for Mirza!

Sarajevo, 30 October 1992

My one and only love,

I shall try to keep calm while writing this letter, even though that will be difficult for a variety of reasons. In the first place, I don't want to burden you with my problems and sorrows because I imagine you are up to your neck in your own. My words are full of bitterness.

If you received my last letter, you will know that I am right on the front line (even if the entire city is a front line, a blood-soaked battlefield) with a rifle in my hand and a helmet on my head. At the moment Sarajevo is the biggest concentration camp in the world where people live from hand to mouth, suffer and die.

The cold is intense, but most certainly it will not be the cold that kills me.

Beyond the front line, up in the hills, everything is different. I stay huddled in the trenches and sometimes I dig them myself and try to keep my head down because we are being fired at all the time by snipers, machine guns, mortars and tanks. While this is going on, you lie in the mud at the bottom of the trench and wait until it's all over.

My darling, I do hope you realize that I think about you always. My darling wife, I hope this madness will soon end and that it will all seem like a bad dream and that I shall be able to embrace you soon and never, ever lose you.

I embrace you, my darling, and kiss you,
Pavle

Sarajevo, 3 November 1992

Our dear Tanja,

Another chance to write to you has cropped up. As I said in my last letter, we have all kinds of problems, and now we are nerving ourselves to face the winter. Your brother is still in hospital with his ulcer and the longer they keep him in the better for him, because there is no glass left in any of his windows, and the living room wall has also been shattered by a grenade which will create a very serious problem when it gets colder. Another reason why he's better off in hospital is that his sons are always at the barracks and he would be at home all alone. We are all much thinner than we used to be, even though we have enough to eat courtesy of humanitarian aid. Nino, my youngest son, is the only one who has not lost weight, because I keep him at home all the time. In fact, if he went out on the street he would run the risk of being enrolled even though he's only fifteen. Safet is well; he's the only one of us who has actually put on weight. I am as busy as before, working and dashing about all over the place. I'm thinner than before, and if all these horrors resulted in nothing worse than a loss of weight it wouldn't be so bad. We could dream about rebuilding our city and making it even more beautiful than before. But unfortunately that won't happen because, with so many young people dead, a whole generation is going to be lost. And even where the few who remain are concerned, when the war is over we shall have to start thinking where to send them – Australia, Canada, perhaps. Who knows? After so much destruction, even if it were to stop today there will be no prospects here for the next ten years.

Only the old people will be left and a generation of cripples unable, as far as I can see, to work. Perhaps this is God's will. But we shall talk about all this when we are able to communicate normally once more.

We think of you continually and embrace you all.

Zela and Amer

Sarajevo, 5 November 1992

My dear daughter,

You can't imagine how excited we were by your phone-call. It was the last thing we were expecting! That was on Sunday, four days ago. We heard your voice but could not understand all you were saying. The main thing was that we heard you were well and you heard that we were alive and well.

All we understood was that you had sent off a parcel and we were enormously glad about that. We are now waiting for it impatiently and that makes the days go faster. Our imprisonment continues, but must end sooner or later. Now that we have electricity and water and food again, our resistance grows stronger too. I manage to do some work and this keeps me occupied and gives me some peace of mind.

We received your letter dated 2 October some time ago, the one in which you told us about your wedding plans. In our situation, a letter like that was the most wonderful thing that could happen. The odd tear, especially of the masculine variety, refused to be held back!!

I'm so happy to hear that you are working at your new design and that it is successful. One of the saddest things I see around me here is the lack of any prospects for the young people and students. From inside Sarajevo, and with little information at our disposal, it is difficult to see what will happen.

I am sad for Bosnia and the Bosnian people who deserved none of this suffering and injustice. The outside world is behaving selfishly and people here find that difficult to accept. The predominating concepts outside are might and financial interest.

Here we are dying.

I have five or six final-year students who are doing everything to complete their theses; they have all decided to go abroad eventually.

Poor young people, here in the Balkans!

My regards to Filippo whom I do not know. I can't wait to see you again.

I embrace you, I love you immeasurably,
your Papa

Sarajevo, 6 November 1992

My only treasure,

I am writing in haste because I have to dash to the front line. I am sending this with a man I know, and I hope he will tell you something more about our miserable life here. I hope you are still in Vela Luka, otherwise all my efforts to get letters to you would be useless, and this would be a catastrophe for me. As it is I live in hope that you have received some of my letters and heard the messages over the radio, telling you that I still live in this madhouse, that I think about you all the time, that I love you and am waiting for this crazy war to end soon so that we shall not be separated ever again.

When I am at the front I use your ribbon to tie my hair back. So you are with me always, even in the trenches, when I am on sentry duty, when I am sinking in the mud, and military operations are much easier with your presence protecting me. I love you, Jelica, I love you. So far sheer good luck has saved my nut; I am really hoping I will last out. Some of us, unfortunately, have not been so lucky, and they are with us no longer. None of this makes any sense, but no one realizes this, or perhaps they choose not to see it.

My darling, I miss you so terribly, I hear nothing about you. I feel completely cut off from all that is dear to me. I ask myself if I shall ever see my child again, and if I shall ever hold you in my arms again. But I still hope that this senseless war will end and that a time will come when we are together once more and can build our joint future, without political intrigues, without gunpowder, without suffering and without death. I live for that day and for the time that is to come.

I embrace you my darling, look after yourself,
Pavle

Sarajevo, 8 November 1992

Dear Mr George Bush,

I implore you to help our Bosnia. I am a refugee from Vogosca, near Sarajevo. I have nothing to eat, nothing to drink, no bed to sleep in, nothing to keep me warm and almost no clothes to wear. The same goes for the other children of my age. We are starting to die.

I implore you to do something to make the war end and stop them firing over our heads. You could help us so much ... so much ...

Help to end this war and we shall be very grateful. You do not know what this is like, or you know something, a little part of all this. You cannot realize the suffering of these people.

In those parts of the country attacked by the Serbs horrible things are happening. They keep killing and torturing people. It is driving us mad. That is why I am begging you to help us.

My name is Edina Sulejmanovic,
I am 12 years old

PLEASE HELP BOSNIA NOW!

Sarajevo, 19 November 1992

My darling, my dearest one,

I am writing this letter because a neighbour is due to leave tomorrow for Slovenia and will pass through Split where he can post it. All my attempts to get out of Sarajevo have come to nothing. The papers were ready, but that was it. You will already have learnt that I have been at the front for a month now, and only get down to the city occasionally for a couple of hours to wash if the water is on, then I tidy the flat and return here.

I went to see a friend of mine in Alifakovac and passed by the restaurant in Bascarsija. Although the roof and front have been damaged by grenades, I was glad to see it open. I remembered, of course, how often we used to go there in happier times.

Last night I was on sentry duty in the trenches, up to my knees in mud and the snow that fell yesterday, covering the mountains around the city. I lit the fire and imagined myself on the banks of the river Neretva, with you. I see you in every flame, I mentally consult you whatever I'm doing, and in the moments of greatest difficulty I think how you would deal with a similar situation and how you would advise me, and then I get very sad.

It is very difficult, my darling, to live without you, and at the same time I'm happy that you are far away from this senselessness, this madness that grips Sarajevo as if with claws. The worst of it is that there is no end in sight. Winter is here, the first snows fell on 12th November, food is becoming ever scarcer, as is water and light and fuel. The city is sealed on all sides simply by mortals and you feel like a prisoner in a concentration camp. What I have done over the past month has been against all my principles.

I stay alert in the mud-filled trench to avoid being killed, and we are being constantly fired at with every kind of weapon of every conceivable calibre, including those forbidden by the various conventions. But who respects conventions? And when they shoot at me I shoot back. I shoot at people I do not hate, I shoot at them only because they shoot at me intending to kill me, and the thought is in my mind that they too have mothers, children, lovers, that they are living beings into whose hands guns have been put against their will.

Mind, I am not afraid. We are doing this as if it were any other job. We try to do it to the best of our ability and to stay alive and so far it has gone well. I am neither a hero nor a coward. I am fighting simply because it is demanded of me at the moment. I am comforted by the thought that I am fighting for our future. I dream, I dream of happier times . . . am I wrong to do so? Where are you? When you are depressed, do you look at my photo like I look at yours? Every now and then I am gripped by the fear of having lost you in this chaos. That would finish me. There would be no way out.

Ivan is telling me to be quick and sends you his warmest regards. Whenever we're together we talk about you. His wife and daughters are also living near Split. My one and only treasure, be happier than me and don't forget me. It would be absurd to tell you not to worry about me.

I embrace you. I love you so much that it hurts. Look after yourself!

Pavle

The following letter was written by a girl in the Sarajevo orphanage to her friends at Igea Marina.

Sarajevo, 24 November 1992

Dear Dragana and all my friends,

First of all, how are you and what are you doing? Here we are getting bored and don't know what to do with ourselves. Dragana, I should never have dreamed of getting a letter from you. I never thought that we should have to write and that we couldn't see each other ever again. When Amel knocked at the door and I rather impatiently asked him what he wanted, he said: 'Open the door, I've got a surprise for you.' When he gave me your letter, I opened it at once. Then I started to jump for joy, because I haven't stopped crying since the day you left. Later I began to spend some time with Melinda. I think I should have gone mad if Melinda hadn't been here: she sort of took the place of the rest of you. Since you went away, each day has been worse than the one before. I'm crying now, while I write this letter, because I can't imagine life without you. You know how fond I was of all of you, and specially of you. As soon as this hateful war is over, or perhaps even earlier, because there is a chance that we may leave before the 28th November 1992, I shall phone my aunt in Germany! Especially if those big boys keep on annoying me. I can't stand it, because I'm the youngest. Wherever I go with Melinda they tease me. Never a day's peace with all these men: they're all quite mad!

I don't know if you heard about Laza being wounded. He's walking on crutches and has got a bit of metal in his leg. Has Danijela heard anything about her mother? I saw the two photos of you that Romela sent to Miroslav. Please, Dragana, take a photo of you all together and send it to me, it would make me feel a little less unhappy. Time drags, and to make it pass more quickly I re-read your letter and the poetry and look at the photos. It's my only pastime. My greatest joy would be to see you again, or else to be hit by a bullet and die. I don't want to go on living. Dragana, believe me, all the time while I'm writing to you I'm crying. And then my back starts to hurt, always at the worst possible moment. I can't, I swear by my mother, stop thinking about you all, and I can't live without you. I wouldn't wish God to give my awful fate to anyone!

I hope this letter gets to you. Dragana, I must stop writing now, besides, I can't think of anything else to say except that if you could actually see our city now, you would faint!

Bye, and all my love,
Melina

Sarajevo, 29 November 1992

My darlings,

You can't imagine my joy when Julija came yesterday with your letters dated 29 October and 21 November. I am so glad that you are well! Pray God that all this is soon over because it is unbearable. At least knowing that you are settled brings a little happiness. I had heard nothing from you since May. Here the battle is non-stop and we can't take any more of it. I sleep in the cellar, which is the only safe place. Kemo and Marjan also sleep in the cellar. We have beds there and we try to keep it warm. It is a dreadful place, but I am hoping that this nightmare will be over before the end of the year.

My dear Zlatko, Sarajevo has taken a terrible beating. Enver and Branko have been wounded and the others have escaped to Zenica. I'm better than I was, I can now walk with the aid of a stick but I am terribly frightened. I can't stop crying.

As for food, we do receive some from the humanitarian aid agencies . . . but no matter. The important thing is that peace should come as quickly as possible. They have all abandoned us. They pass their resolutions, but the criminals are still up there on the mountains firing their big guns at the city, especially at the weekend when reinforcements arrive and they are joined by mercenaries.

Only the thought that you are safe and that whatever happens some of us will survive makes me happy and gives me some hope that we shall be together again some day. How are my little granddaughters? I can't wait for our soldiers to see these criminals off so that my babies can return to their own home.

Don't spend out money on food parcels for us, we receive humanitarian aid like everyone else. The worst of it is that winter has arrived and we are without water, light and gas, but we hope we'll survive. The important thing is that the children are away from here and safe. We have no information about the house in Ilidza because the Chetniks are there.

Write to us, we love you very much,

Papa, Mamma and Uncle Kemo

Sarajevo, 29 November 1992

My dear children and grandchildren,

There is no end to this nightmare. I should love to be with you, but given the present situation that is impossible. However, we live in the hope that there will be an end to it, even if our strength is exhausted and we are becoming impatient. How are you all? Do write more often because it would give us so much pleasure. Thank you for your parcel, it arrived just in time. The shooting is continuous here and it is impossible to leave the house. So far the winter has not been very cold and we are bearing up. We wish this nightmare would end so that we could see you again if nothing else.

We send you enormous hugs,
Mamma

Sarajevo, 30 November 1992

My dears,

How are you? How are my granddaughters Una and Jasna? What are they doing? How are you living and how are you managing for money? Has Zlatko been able to find a job? Your messages arrived all together yesterday. We also received a message from Haso and Enesa in Mostar. Enesa sent us 10 German marks. We keep asking about your parcel but are told that it hasn't arrived yet, and, given the situation, I'm afraid that it probably never will now. Don't send me anything else unless I ask you to do so. Ten days ago we also received a letter from Aida in London, and she says that you and she have been in touch. We were extremely surprised that Aida should have turned up unexpectedly in London and at that point we were not sure where you were. Lots of hugs to my dear, beautiful granddaughters. Their grandmother and I can't wait to see them again. Luckily we have their photographs, and look at them constantly. We tell each other that it is a great blessing for them not to be here surrounded by these horrors. Tell the girls that after many attempts their friends Mak and Darjan have been able to leave the city at last and we hope that they are now in Prague.

All good wishes,
your grandfather

Sarajevo, 30 November 1992

Yesterday was 'Republika' Day . . . I haven't written to you for months and months. I don't know what to write and I don't want to repeat myself. We are living and working and often dawn arrives before we put the candles out in our room. I am living with my 'husband' in Borko. For the moment we have enough food to keep us alive. As for vitamins, I only hope I don't need to take them.

The war continues. I can honestly tell you that everything I've said seems stupid and boringly mundane. In fact worse than that, it seems normal! This is the saddest part of it all, that one gets used to it.

Little by little I'm forgetting what it's like to shop at the supermarket, to buy eggs, mayonnaise, meat; not to have to pay in German marks for the little one gets, and to have something left over to live on – not to mention the little extras. Oh dear! What a whinger!

I feel like Ziggie Stardust, an alien from another planet. I want nothing more from life than to get the hell away from this bloody city that is no longer Sarajevo. It is no longer our own dear Sarajevo.

When all's said and done, this is a ROCK'N'ROLL number!

Give my regards to our friends in Israel if you are still in touch with them.

I often dream about them. And I dream about you, and I dream about the sea.

Regards to the others. We're still alive, thank God, and more or less healthy.

Lada

Sarajevo, 2 December 1992

Dear brother,

We received your letter last week, the first we've had since June. We wept with joy to know that you realize what is going on here and that you are thinking of us. Those tears seemed to lift a weight from my heart, and I feel better now.

Dear Jasmin, the situation is very difficult here, but we are all hoping that it will soon be over and that we shall survive. We have become accustomed to the noise of grenades, to gunfire, dead bodies, bombs. Our most difficult job is staying out of harm's way. Everything else comes a poor second. Thanks to the parcel delivered by the journalists together with your letter, we had a banquet of a kind that is rare indeed here: roast potatoes and tinned meat. We had no seasoning, but it was still much tastier than our usual fare, boiled rice or pasta. Sometimes I manage to find an onion, then I cut it into pieces and it gives a little flavour to our food for at least a week. We miss green vegetables, fruit and seasonings very much. The aid parcels sometimes contain a real treasure such as a box of matches, sweets or a roll of toilet paper. Luckily Papa left us some provisions when he left. Black market goods, which are scarce anyway, are dreadfully expensive and you can only buy them with German marks. A packet of cigarettes costs ten marks fifty, a litre of oil twenty-five. I haven't got a job; I'm on the waiting list. I get two thousand Bosnian dinars a month and with that I can buy half a kilo of pasta – if I can find it. Even bread is difficult to find. We have been without water and without light for a long time now and it is dreadful. Luckily your brother-in-law has managed to provide us with some drinking water from headquarters, and for flushing the toilet we collect water from puddles in the street whenever it rains.

My dear brother, one can get used to anything if one has no choice. I send you my dearest love,

Amela

Sarajevo, 3 December 1992

Dear Kenan,

It is snowing. For the first time this year, luckily. You will remember some years when the snow arrived as early as October.

I am at the office, which is of course cold, unheated, freezing; another typical wartime day in Sarajevo. The usual humiliating and primitive routine: a 'shower' with a damp flannel, a hasty donning of clothes and then a 'wider view' from the news on the radio. There is no other dimension to life. You wake up to nothingness, by half past four in the afternoon it is dark, you sit by a candle until 'late' – nine o'clock – and so to bed. And all the time, from far and near, the noise of gunfire. I am not trying to paint a picture of depression. This is simply how it is. This is our destiny. But I did want to try to describe my sense of the fall of this city, of its men, of this country, into an abyss of misery and impotence. No electricity, no water, no telephones, no heating.

But I have now realized something that I never knew before, that I could not have imagined: men never give up. Those whom until yesterday we would have written off as good for nothing you now see searching for wood, lighting fires, carrying heavy drums of water over great distances, simply facing up to disaster.

Life in wartime has stripped them and transformed them into 'primitive man'. Let me describe one incident that sums it all up. On exactly the same spot where, not very long ago, policemen clutching walkie-talkies were awaiting the former president of Bosnia-Hercegovina, that same former president and his wife are standing today, bundled up in thick clothes, tending a fire laid between two bricks, preparing their food and coffee and breaking off little branches. As you see, everything has changed.

Yours, Sefik

Sarajevo, 5 December 1992

My dear daughter Ana,

What a striking contrast we have again between your letter, which is all joy, and our reply, which is the reality.

This time, your own handwriting was on the envelope (your last letter arrived in a special UNHCR envelope). I did not open it immediately, not knowing your situation and fearing what the contents might be. Then I opened it. I read about your trip to Grado. I don't know if you can possibly grasp how far away from us all these beautiful and jolly things are. Streetlights, bright neon signs, children laughing out loud . . . I didn't know whether to laugh with joy because there is still a world out there totally different from ours and because you, my daughter, can go for a walk without fear of snipers and my grandson can enjoy an ice cream. Or cry with despair over the immeasurable stupidity of men and their destructive instinct.

And now I'll tell you about our situation, which I might describe metaphorically as follows: over our heads hangs a bomb that is worse than the atomic bomb. An atomic bomb, as you know, kills in three ways, by explosion, by heat and by radiation. So anyone who has such a bomb thinks twice before using it.

The bomb hanging everlastingly over us kills first by artillery fire, then by the approach of winter and lastly by starvation.

All three stages of our bomb are already activated and the effects become daily more intense.

You must forgive me for the pessimism pervading my letters, which has its roots not only in what is happening now, but also in my personal disillusionment. Because I could never have dreamt, not in my worst nightmares, that a war, a war like this, was possible in Sarajevo, in our own, in my own, Sarajevo.

I have tried to look at life from a different angle (perhaps it's too late at sixty-five?). I look at other people and see what they do. I see people trying to survive, to adapt to circumstances, even to profit from them. Some people have indeed succeeded in making a great deal of money.

Then there are able people, with initiative. I should like to emulate the latter, but have no direction, no plan. I wasn't prepared for this.

Should I stay or should I leave Sarajevo (supposing it to be possible)?

I don't know what will happen to you and I don't know what to do with your brother Dario.

Should we go away for a time? Or for ever?

I have only just realized the full significance of the term 'Balkan powderkeg' . . . and shall do all I can to get Dario away from here. But where to? Should I perhaps send him to Uncle Milos in America, or to Aunt Stela in Australia?

I don't know.

With all my love,
Papa

Sarajevo, 5 December 1992

Dear children,

Everything here continues to deteriorate. So much that was part of our lives and that we loved has now disappeared. Some images of this tragedy you took with you when you left, having lived through the early stages. And you will probably have met people who left after you and who will have described the terrible things that happened to them. I am sure that you have been sharing our trials from afar.

I have no intention of dwelling on such things. All I want is to see you again as soon as possible, or at least to hear your voices on the phone, since I know that for you and for us this is all that is necessary to make us feel like normal human beings once more.

I should like to be able to convince you that there is no need to worry about us or about all those still here who are dear to you. The strength of character people show in adapting to circumstances is quite incredible. I should explain that life here, after the first months of practice in coping with danger, goes on quite normally. People go out, go to work nearly every day, receive humanitarian aid, meet their friends, even go occasionally to a bar despite the fact that there is nothing to drink. What can we hope for? We must hope for the best. Every war, but especially one like this, forces people to change to some extent. But most of the people who were good and honest will stay that way, even under fire. Unscrupulous people, with no character or morals, will become worse in a war. But, my dears, I want to assure you that when you eventually see those who are dear to you once more, you will not be disappointed.

Your father

Sarajevo, 14 December 1992

My darlings,

It was exactly eight months ago that you set off, very apprehensively, on your 'excursion'. You disappeared round the corner at the top of the stairs.

I can still see that so clearly in my mind's eye that it seems only a few days ago. And yet the time has been long indeed, for time, these days, strikes cruel blows.

I am sitting in the living room that has, over the last two days, undergone the latest in a long line of changes. As I probably told you in a previous letter, we borrowed an ancient oil-burning stove and, since it is now almost impossible to find any oil, we have converted it to burn wood, which though scarce is still available. So the stove has become – as in most apartments – the focal point around which everything revolves. We have, indeed, given it pride of place in the middle of the room.

We took the old furniture from Kenan's study, the armchair from my room and the old white rug and blankets from the bedroom, and put them all in here. So we now have a place that looks really nice and cosy, especially when the stove is burning brightly.

Your letter was delivered last night by the Italian pacifists. Their arrival was quite a moving event, reminding us for a whole day what it feels like to be in touch with the rest of the world. When we first saw them, in such numbers, we couldn't believe our eyes. When they started to produce letters from their rucksacks it never crossed my mind that there would be one for us too. We were so delighted, more than you can imagine. To us these pacifists seemed like supernatural beings that had descended from another planet to our incredibly gloomy, devastated city. People regarded them certainly with gratitude for their good will and enthusiasm, but also with amazement, like adults watching children perform heroic deeds.

Perhaps we have grown tired of speeches of solidarity and support in a world where nothing changes.

Semir met some of them and gave them the letter for you together with your phone number. How are we living? Well, I have to admit that we have gradually adapted ourselves and now live this strange life as if it had always been so. We don't think very much about what is happening around us, but just try to solve our daily problems. We read. Every now and then I translate something, invariably on a subject totally unrelated to the war, and wait for the time when my translations will once again be of interest to someone. I should have liked to do more, but it would have meant taking an enormous risk that, in my opinion, would not have been warranted by the result. I believe it is better to be patient and to save one's strength for what may happen later.

I hope, however, that the worst is now over.

Even this dreadful year is on its way out!

When one of us leaves the house the other two worry very much. But to worry over that with everything else that is happening is a superfluous emotion.

Semir is working exceedingly hard. He and his computer are engaged in a 'battle' with the power cuts in order to finish his thesis. The last cut came just as he was putting the final touches. As soon as the thesis is done he will, it seems, have a proper job in the computer room at the hospital. This, he tells me, is the job he has always dreamed of. So currently he is dashing about between the Red Cross, the clinic and the university where he and his professor are working on a project together.

In normal times this would all have been a source of great joy.

The Renault 5 has been very badly affected by the war. The combined ravages of thieves, bullets and shrapnel have almost completely written it off. But the things that are happening around us are too terrible for this to be of any importance.

Nebojsa and Vesna often come to see us, to our great delight. Nebojsa has been appointed editor-in-chief at the radio station, Vesna complains because she never sees him and he, as always, just smiles!

Sometimes he stops off at Damir's on his way back, has a drink to toast the birth of the baby, and then gets home after the start of the curfew. You can imagine what Vesna has to say about that! But the two of them are trying to keep their relationship calm and serene despite the situation, and they are always a delight when they come here.

As for the rest, my dear Sanja, our entire philosophy faculty has had to squeeze into one small room at the end of one of the innumerable passages in the law school. The few teachers and lecturers that remain meet once a week, but we discuss nothing except humanitarian aid or how to provide for the winter.

When all this is over we shall have to start rebuilding our lives from scratch in every little detail.

There are even some who are enjoying their greatest moment of success at this very time, as, for example, Jevdja. You may have heard that Slavko Pervan has staged the famous musical *Hair* with a group of artists. Music is so lovely, it is one of the few things that can inspire confidence and optimism even in the midst of total destruction. Children go to see *Hair* ten or fifteen times. Jevdja, who has one of the principal parts, has become a real star. He has quite naturally become identified with the role, and struts around the city with teenage girls swarming round making a fuss of him.

I don't know whether Mamma has already told you about our new tenant, who is showing signs of life at this very moment. This is Kico, Semir's parrot and a refugee from Dobrinja. He's just like our old Cici and we all adore him. Papa is always roaming round the house trying to find the warmest spot for him. The only thing that makes me sad is to think that my little Zlatan has never seen him, because he is an incredibly intelligent bird and can already pronounce his own name faultlessly. Kico also shares our 'rustic idyll', our living room. I'm telling you all this so that you can picture us more easily.

We meet Nihad very often; he's always travelling between Mojmilo and the centre of town. He has seen and lived through so much, yet has lost none of his calm and confidence. I am not even going to attempt to describe his reactions when your parcel arrived. He was speechless, and it was only his black eyes, shining with excitement and joy, that gave him away. And his son Fedja, obviously very moved, expressed a wish that you would 'live for a hundred years'.

In the hope that things will settle down eventually, we are going to try to reopen the offices sometime in the next few days. At the moment this is not possible; for one thing, with no electricity not even the telephones in Sarajevo are working. Everything is cold and empty. Of course Irfan Durmic, general manager of the electricity company, has become the most famous media person around over the last few months. His communiqués and reports about repairs to the electricity cables are listened to as often as five times a day. Even General Morillon and the bulletins from

Geneva are relegated to second place. When Irfan Durmic speaks you can hear a pin drop!!!

Now that the long-awaited chance of sending you a letter has finally arrived, there are so many things I want to say that my thoughts are chasing each other around and my mind has gone blank. Often, in my thoughts, I write to you and speak to you, but when I pick up a pen and try to sort out the chaos in my head, it seems much more difficult. All that matters is that we love each other and give each other all the support we can. This is the only way we shall succeed in filling these strange days and making them bearable.

You must believe me when I tell you that we are all well, that we all look after each other, that we are careful and coping with all the problems reasonably well. I can't say that our experiences are pleasant ones, but let's hope that it will all be over soon.

When we look around and see everyone else is in a similar situation, that we are all in the same boat, the problems become easier to bear and simpler to overcome.

In Sarajevo at present everyone is trying to help everyone else, and this is the nicest thing out.

I don't need to say how much we miss you. I particularly love Saturdays and Sundays because then I can picture you where you are. But even this will eventually be a thing of the past, and we shall have all the time in the world to talk.

And many things, I hope, will be forgotten.

Take great care of yourselves, and give our adored Zlatan a kiss every time you think of us.

We send you lots of hugs and lots of love,

Mia

Sarajevo, 17 December 1992

My dears,

I don't know what you've heard from other members of the family.
For myself, I never go out and can only try to describe one of my
'working days'.

The day begins in the dark and ends in the dark, and that is no
allegory because we go to bed at seven and get up in the morning
at five when it is still dark. Night falls while we are having our
supper, at three in the afternoon. We spend the short daylight
hours preparing food, looking for water and hunting for some
kind of illumination, etc. At midday the race is on to find a
'slot' in the communal kitchen. The other day I counted no
less than nine saucepans on the go at the same time. There are
in fact nine tenants, not counting visiting friends. No one ever
removes their shoes now, and I can't even remember what our
red carpet looks like, you remember, the one of which I used to
be so proud!

So then, all round the communal kitchen, the discussions start.
We ask each other's opinion about questions of strategy, bitterly
criticise the futility and time-wasting of the diplomatic manoeuvres
and thus it can sometimes happen that even the little food procured
with such effort gets burnt.

I have to admit to being very sad about the fate of the trees in
the garden, but I take comfort from the fact that I have finished
all the preparation in the vegetable plot. Granny and I never go
out unless it is really unavoidable, so we have plenty of time to
argue. We listen to the news on a little radio that runs off the car
battery, because there are no ordinary batteries left. Granny makes
a delicious black bread with bran mixed into it, which is supposed
to be very good for one.

I am writing to you by the light of an oil lamp; it works very
well, which is more than can be said for tallow candles, which
burn my fingers. The thing I miss most at the moment is a red
onion, and our dinner is on the meagre side. A few days ago I
saw a photograph of a man eating a slice of fat bacon and it
reminded me of the past and how silly I was to eat such
fatty food.

My dears, I shall have to stop. My glasses are misting up because the temperature in the room has reached 15 degrees, not bad at all in the present circumstances.

My love to you all,
Grandfather

Sarajevo, 18 December 1992

Dear Silvia,

Your letter came as a great surprise after hearing nothing for eight months. When I opened it, believe me, it was quite a while before I could read it through the tears that filled my eyes. I was disappointed, however, to hear that you have received none of my letters, although I have written at least seven or eight times and have given the letters to people who could leave Sarajevo, begging them to take them and post them wherever possible. I even sent a message over the radio. As for us, we are still alive and that is all that matters in this hell. We live one day at a time and are satisfied when the day ends and we are still alive. Every day is the same as the one before, and we no longer notice that they pass one after the other, with no point and no chance of being able to do anything. All we think about is saving our skins, because here life is cheap, it costs no more than a single bullet. And bullets fly about our city like flocks of birds, from one apartment block to another, from one pavement to another. We pass the days in a state of semi-stupor; we hear bombs exploding and wonder what else has been destroyed, and in the evening we congratulate each other – aloud – on the fact that another day is over. Then we congratulate ourselves – silently – for still being alive. The worst part of it is having no water or electricity. It is impossible to wash or to cook. Our clothes we wash in cold water, when we can find any, and forget about ironing. It is like a ghost city with no shops, no supermarkets. We are mentally worn out. We use everything we can to light a fire: benches, tables, chairs, timbers from bombed-out buildings, shelving from the shops, old furniture, trees from the parks and avenues.

But do not worry about us, because we are not alone in our plight. We are all in the same boat, and this gives us courage and we all hope that better times are on the way.

Think of us and do not forget us,
Seka

Sarajevo, 20 December 1992

My darlings,

This is the fourth letter that I have written to you and I have not had a single reply. I have heard nothing more about you. I don't know if you got my letters, how you are, or if you are still in Rimini. The journalists I gave the letters to promised to take them out of Sarajevo and post them to you, but perhaps you are no longer at the same address. I wrote to you to tell you that Granny died on 22 September and that during her last days she spoke of you all the time and was very sad that you were not here. There has been no change in the situation, we are still hemmed in, prisoners in the city, and there is firing all around. There is now another problem: the winter. We can no longer go down to the cellar because we have been turned out by the rats . . . it is now their domain.

The cold is unbearable. I can't tell you how much I miss you. I think of you all the time and don't know if you think of me. Azra, we missed you so much when Granny died. We managed to give her a proper funeral although this has now become so difficult here and there was no coffin to be had. We buried her in the mosque near our home. Anur and Tanja, remember to be good and do what Mummy tells you. This is the best possible present you can give Daddy. Azra, do teach our language to your little brother and sister. Do whatever you can to help them remember it even though they are growing up in an Italian-speaking country. I remember you more vividly with every day that passes, and every day makes me long for you more. I wish you all a happy Christmas and a happy New Year. I can't wait for all this to end.

Daddy

Winter 1992–1993

Please
STOP the war
in Croatia and Bosnia

December 1992
First severe cold in Sarajevo. Many old people die in the hospice at Nedzarici. The temperature falls to minus 20°C. The city is still without water, light, gas and telecommunications.

December 1992/January 1993
The Vance-Owen plan for the division of Bosnia-Hercegovina into 10 provinces is discussed in Geneva. The plan is accepted in its entirety by the Bosnian Croats, while the Moslems only agree to the constitutional proposals, as does the Assembly of the self-proclaimed Serbian Republic in Pale.

9 January
Hakija Turajlic, vice-president of the Bosnian government, is killed while travelling in a UN tank.

9 and 10 January
Ecumenical conference in Assisi, where the atrocities committed in Bosnia-Hercegovina are condemned. The Pope celebrates a mass for Bosnia-Hercegovina.

Fighting has continued throughout the month between Croat and Moslem forces in central Bosnia.

14 February
Humanitarian flights leave Ancona (Falconara) for Sarajevo. The new air-bridge replaces that from Zagreb which has now become unsafe due to fighting in the area.

16 and 17 February
Bernard Henry-Levy's documentary film *Un jour dans la mort de Sarajevo* is shown at the Berlin Film Festival.

19 February
President Izetbegovic declares a unilateral ceasefire on all fronts.

22 February
UN Resolution 808 formally sets up the war crimes tribunal proposed on 31 October 1992.

1 March
The USA, under the auspices of the UN, starts to drop humanitarian aid by parachute into the besieged towns of eastern Bosnia.

5 March
A woman working for the humanitarian organization Equilibre is killed, and two men wounded, in Sarajevo.

12 March
General Morillon leaves Sarajevo with a small military escort for the besieged city of Srebrenica where the situation is desperate.

15 March
General Morillon decides to remain in Srebrenica as a hostage until the arrival of humanitarian aid.

22 March
Sarajevo is subjected to extremely heavy bombing. According to data gathered by the UN, no less than 2,398 bombs have fallen on the city.

24 March
Radovan Karadzic unexpectedly abandons the peace conference in New York, rejecting the Vance-Owen Plan.

29 March
General Morillon returns to Sarajevo from Belgrade where he had been involved in peace negotiations with the Serbs.

Sarajevo, 21 December 1992

Dear Mrs . . .

This is the first time I have had an opportunity of writing to you.
A television crew (working for Antenne 2) has been filming our
Institute of Romance Languages in the deserted university, with its
wrecked lecture theatres and broken windows, at a temperature of
−3°. But this is only a part of the picture. The reality, unfortunately,
is much worse. At dawn this morning the temperature was −13°.
There is no water, heating or electricity in the city. From the
earliest hours of the morning one sees nothing but the spectral
forms of human beings that were once men and women, once
Europeans, passing by in the semi-darkness on their search for a
little water and a few twigs. All the parks and public gardens have
disappeared. Where there used to be beautiful gardens now there
are bare patches where you see nothing but stumps. Why has this
happened? Why have some people assumed the right, as Hannah
Arendt put it, of '. . . deciding who may and who may not inhabit
this planet?' What have they become, those who were our friends
and brothers?

As for me, I have nothing left. My house has gone, and so has
my library of five thousand volumes that I loved in the true sense
of the word, and which was such a source of pride. Sometimes
I dream that I am in the library, leafing through books that fall
open at the well-thumbed pages.

But 'There is no greater sorrow than the recollection of a happy
time in misery,' as Dante says. I remember all those days I spent
at Inalco and in the university town that for me is no longer part
of the real world. Something that still exists has retreated into the
irrecoverable past since twenty four million kilograms of iron, steel
and explosives fell upon Sarajevo.

And yet we live, we live intensely, as if the whole of our life
were crystallized into these few terrible, yet at the same time
sublime, months. We organized our 'Sepharad 92' in memory of
the arrival of the Jews in Bosnia, and celebrated the five hundredth
anniversary without pomp but in a fitting manner.

We have no electricity, only little lamps that illuminate our cold
rooms with a gloomy light. But am I not a mediaevalist when
all's said and done, so why should I not work like a monk of

the Middle Ages? We write in spite of everything. In our sadness there are moments of intense joy, because we are conscious of being alive, even if our existence is constantly threatened by all that is happening around us.

I now live in a small apartment riddled with bullet-holes and scarred by shells; it was lent to me by a Jewish family. Every item of my clothing is on loan from someone. So much the better: omnia mea mecum porto!

My book has been printed at last and I have a copy for you and your husband. I should be very happy to teach again one day at Inalco and in your institute. Would you put in a word for me with those who decide these matters? Vanitas vanitatem! I have spoken too much about myself and have omitted to ask about you. As the festive season is now with us, I should like to wish you a happy Christmas and to send you my best wishes for the coming New Year, that it may bring you and your family all that you desire.

As always, . . .

Sarajevo, 22 December of the war year 1992

My adored and distant star,

After three days of violent fighting I have returned from the field of battle, tired, soaked, covered in mud, but happy because I am still in one piece and because I know that you are there, somewhere, my hope, my dream that will become reality when this mayhem is over. You are coming to seem like a mythical being to whom I can turn in difficult moments, in whom I can believe, seeking shelter and warmth. I continue to wonder whether you get my letters. A letter from you would mean peace of mind, balm, elixir. I miss you, I miss you terribly, my dearest being. Sometimes shivers run down my spine at the thought of holding you in my arms, being close to you, being enveloped in your warmth, of closing my eyes, relaxing and forgetting . . . Darling, I'm weary, and there is no rest. I have been fighting in the hills around the city for days, in the snow and mud, against an enemy I do not hate, because I do not know how to hate, an enemy that I regard like the monster in the fairy stories that must be hacked to pieces with the sword, the impenetrable forest around the castle of Sleeping Beauty. I believe with all my heart that I shall emerge from these shadows and shall come to you, so delicate, luminous, dear, but the carelessness or tiredness of an instant, or even bad luck, could check me for ever.

My darling, should they force me to my knees, should they prove themselves stronger than me, then know this, when I am no more, that I have loved you with a pure and honest love, an enormous love.

Be happy, I embrace you, my love,
Pavle

Sarajevo, 23 December 1992

Our dearest treasure,

We have all gathered together to write this letter to you and tell you that for the moment we are all safe and sound. True, Papa and Grandad are very thin, but no matter; Papa only weighs sixty-six kilos and looks like a teenager. One thing we must tell you, Bruno, is that Papa is now on sentry duty at Stup, just down the road, so you can tell your friends in Milan that your father is a hero. He comes home every two or three days bringing wood and coal, and when we see him he reminds us of the 'snowman in the sun' of the fairy tales. He's growing a beard, but apart from that he hasn't changed at all. When he comes home we all swarm round him asking questions by the dozen, and he replies reluctantly saying that all's quiet at Stup, there's no shooting and the only problem is lack of food. So you see you needn't worry about him because he's just the same as ever.

Mamma is well and hasn't lost any weight because she and I are the ones who eat the most. She's become a great cook. She can make a tin of meat and half a kilo of rice into a meal that lasts for three days. The one thing she didn't want to cook for me was 'pita'.* We badgered her for ten days and in the end she relented and made some, and Ado and I ate every bit of it. There's no water supply and no electric light, but for water we manage alright as the only available water in the Alipasino area is in our cellar, so all we have to do is go down and get it. I forgot to tell you that Mamma has lots of neighbours and they spend all their time together. Occasionally she has a fit of the weepies, but then calms down again. It's more difficult for Grandad. He's always on his own. He lights the fire and we've dubbed him 'head stoker' because he does it better than anyone else. I almost forgot to tell you one big news item: Amira, Mirza and Zijada have returned from Kolonija.* Eso went to fetch them so they were able to cross the airport road. They are well because they were living better there than they would have here.

*Pita: very thin puff-pastry stuffed with spinach, meat, cheese, etc.
*Kolonija: a suburb of Sarajevo, near Butmir airport. The first to be heavily shelled, it has never fallen into Serb hands.

I've told you about everyone else but nothing about me, and now there's no time because it's my 'turn of duty'. I've been 'head of the household' since Papa has been away. The only problem is that no one listens to me. I'm responsible for fetching water and firewood. Sometimes I play the guitar and I've got very good, so you may see me some day on the television in Milan (I'm only joking). When you get back I'll teach you to play the guitar, too. Now that it's not quite so cold I go out sometimes. The greatest thing that has happened to me since the war started was Sanela's birthday party. There was food and drink, we played the harmonica and danced. It was super.

Now I'll tell you how we've managed for firewood. We bought ten plum trees from a little old lady for fifty German marks, and Mamma helped us to chop them up.

I really can't think of anything else to write about. Don't worry about us, study hard, enjoy yourself and think how lucky you are to be safe.

Write to us if you can and tell us about your school and how you get on with your new friends.

With love from all of us,
your brother Ole, Papa, Mamma, and Grandpa

Sarajevo, Christmas Eve 1992

My love, my love, my love,

You have given me the perfect Christmas present. Your letter, your long-awaited letter. My darling, as all hell has broken loose around here, I've made out my will. Just to be on the safe side, even though I have no intention of dying as yet. But times being what they are, and no one knowing what the outcome will be, I wanted to play safe. Try to do everything in accordance with the will: it's very important that no one else should have our lovely apartment. So please don't sell it. If I survive, which I fully intend to do, I'll think what to do with it later. My love, it's so strange to be writing to you about such things, but I have been here for months with a gun in my hand, in the hills around the city, fighting for something better, for a happy future. You know what I think about the war, but it was the only thing to do.

Maybe if you could see what remains of my native city, if you knew how many dear friends are no longer with us, you would understand. On top of which, the enemy has come between the two of us and prevents me from taking you in my arms and kissing you. This cannot be allowed to continue. For the moment I am intact . . . oh, pardon me, not quite intact. A bullet passed through my thigh and I have received a commendation for bravery. The bullet went right through from one side to the other and the commendation is all that remains – apart from the scars. I quite agree that we shall come out of this mayhem as changed people and that nothing will be the same again. But one thing you must understand, that you are always with me, day and night, at every moment; and that whatever I do I do it only for us. When I'm in action I tie my hair back (this will amuse you) with your black velvet ribbon, and I carry the locket (you know what is inside it) round my neck, so you do not leave me even for an instant. You watch over me. I miss you so much that I ache with longing. If something should happen to me, you mustn't be sad, my darling, and try, when it becomes possible, to bury me near my parents so that we are together again as before. It makes me very sad to hear how difficult things are for you and not to be able to help you. I know that living in Croatia is very expensive. Be brave and sensible, because with your ability and your experience I know you'll be able to find a job.

Now I'll tell you something about life here. Sarajevo is a concentration camp, the biggest ghetto in the world. Apart from corpses, which we have in abundance, we have nothing. We have had no water and no light for two months, only promises of reconnection. This very morning, as it was Christmas Eve, I had a shower under a jet of warm promises. You can't imagine how I enjoyed it. The barter system is thriving as it did in the good old days. For five packets of cigarettes you can get a hand-grenade that solves the food problem at a stroke. You lie on it, pull out the pin and all your problems are solved definitively – apart from disposing of the remains. This winter the problem of heating has been solved by our enemies. Every day they burn a few apartment buildings, museums or other useless edifices, depending on how they happen to feel, so that people can warm themselves without fuss at the flames of their own home, school, kindergarten, hospital, etc. Prices have a logic all their own. Seeing that we are moving towards Europe and that Europe, as we all know, is an old lady and naturally slow on her feet, we have overtaken her as far as values, products and services are concerned. (Pardon me, there are no services, we don't need them.) My present salary is 70,000 plus a small military supplement of 20,000, which together make up 90 German marks, certainly not enough to live on.

But anyway, what can I, or what should I buy with such a sum, seeing that there is already such a superabundance of everything? If I do decide to spend some money, I could buy, let us say, a sack of freshly-cut wood, not for heating since we are all hot enough, but in memory of, and compassion for, what once formed the green lungs of our city. This is how it is, my darling, in the capital city of the youngest internationally recognized sovereign republic in the world.

As it is Christmas Eve tonight (and I have fasted for a long time), I have decided to dine in style in a way entirely consonant with the dictates of our faith – on three slices of bread liberally soaked in vividly-coloured rainwater.

In closing, my distant star of hope, I wish you joy in 1993.

Pavle

Sarajevo, 26 December 1992

Dear Aunt,

We haven't been able to write to you for ages because nothing, not even a bird, could get into or out of Sarajevo. The airport was closed and also the road from Kiseljak where the fighting was very fierce, and this meant that not one gramme of food could get through to Sarajevo. It seems impossible to us that no one can help us, and we cannot believe it. There is shooting from all sides, and even those who are 'on our side' punish us by not bringing anything to eat. But no one can think straight any more and whatever happens we have to accept it as we have no other choice. The situation here does not change, and the hardest thing to bear is that nothing is moving. We have already been without water and power for three weeks. It has been terrible. During the summer we noticed it less, because it was warm and there was plenty of daylight, but it is very cold now. The cold gets right into your bones even if you wear three sweaters, three pairs of socks and three pairs of trousers around the house. People looking like zombies wander, or rather scurry, around the city clutching containers and bags and looking for water and firewood. And no one now takes any notice of the shells falling around them or snipers' bullets, because they only have the one idea in their minds, how to feed themselves and keep themselves warm. Every tree in the city, in every park, avenue and cemetery, has been cut down, so, besides being a bombed and burnt-out city, we shall also be a treeless city. And no one lifts a finger. In the hospitals, the old people and children suffer dreadfully from the cold because there are not enough blankets even for them. Terrible. Terrible. There are times when I think I am going mad, and I wonder how other people find the strength to carry on . . .

Nadira

Sarajevo, 28 December 1992

Dear Grandpa, Uncle, Aunt and Jasmina,

How are you? We are well. Dear Grandpa, Sanja and I can't wait to see you again. We love you very, very much. How lucky you are to live somewhere where there is peace!

Where have all those happy days gone? Who could ever have guessed that there would be a war and we would have to write letters to you. How is Jasmina?

Grandpa, when do you think we shall be able to go for one of our walks together again? I can't wait to see you again. Sanja has grown and has learnt to write the alphabet and numbers and to read a little. She has lost her first little tooth. We were so glad that you managed to get out of Banja Luka. As soon as you have a chance to come here, we shall be waiting for you impatiently and will be so happy.

If you can, please send us a parcel of food because we are hungry.

We wish you a happy New Year. We also wish Jasmina a happy birthday in peace, not in war like us.

Take care, we love you,
Maja and Sanja
[*aged 10 years and 4 years*]

Sarajevo, 1 January 1993

Dear Papa, Jasmin, Vesna and Jasmina,

As you see, we have seen the new year in at war. We must pray to God and ask him to prevent another year like this. It was a horrible year without you, Papa, and all the others, and without electricity and water. I'm sure your New Year's Eve was a jollier affair than ours, but you must have been anxious about us. Don't worry, we are still fine, thank God. We have got some firewood and can at least keep warm. Jasminska has gone back to her apartment in Dobrinja with her daughters and they are heating the place with diesel fuel. We never received the parcel from Azra and don't even know where we can go to look for it. Send a parcel if you can.

With love from us all,
Seka and Granny

Mamma wants to add a couple of words:

Dear Jasmin, my dear son,

It is very difficult here especially for us old people, but let's hope that the young ones, at least, can hold out. As for myself, I slept with your sister in the cellar for three months. In the cellar we often heard nothing but a deathly silence. When we heard shooting, we were terrified and our hearts would begin to pound more and more, not with joy but with sadness. Our hearts were weeping, though their tears were invisible. Every now and then we could hear, in the silence, the sobs of children.

My dear son, it is very cold and I doubt if I shall survive, because I am much weakened and now only weigh 48 kilograms. Dear Jasmin, I don't know if we shall ever meet again, and if we don't, forgive me if I have ever offended you by word or deed. Think of your sister and do not forget her because she chose to stay here and help me, and is the one who has suffered most of all you young people.

Dear Jasmin, you must not send us money because we have sufficient for our needs and now that your father is with you you will need it yourself.

I send you my dearest wishes and embrace you all.

Mamma Fika

Sarajevo, 2 January 1993

Dear cousins and grandchildren,

An English journalist has offered to take this letter. He is going to
Belgrade and told me that he would send it to you in Milan.

Here everything is as it was. The cold continues to get worse and
the shooting in the hills is relatively light, but you will know what
I mean by relatively. We only receive one kilo of bread a week, so
I have tried to adapt the boiler and make an oven. But it needs
firewood. Your aunt, who was such a robust woman, has shrunk
to half her size and I am afraid that the bombardment and all these
horrors have driven her out of her mind. When I leave home in the
morning to go and look for firewood, she kneels in front of the
door, and when I get back in the evening I find her in the same
position. The nearest place for getting water is three kilometres
away, and one has to start queueing at dawn in order to have a
hope of getting any, so I am out for hours at a time. But what
else can I do? We are old, and even if we could get out of here,
where would we go? How could we live? We no longer have any
money, and we cannot work, so what have we to hope for?

Sometimes, when I go looking for wood, I stay hidden in the
ruins for hours waiting for those who are younger and stronger
than me to take what they want first, because I could not compete
with them. Then I take whatever is left, and I remember that before
this war started I had a job and a respectable life and now I'm only
an old man who has to rummage through the rubbish. Then I bless
my sister for having given birth to two daughters who have made
a life for themselves in Italy and are safe . . .

Take great care of yourselves. A big hug,
Grandad Nermin

Sarajevo, 6 January 1993

Dear Laura,

As I was sending your birthday card, I thought it was a good chance to write a letter as well. I sent you a letter a few days ago, but I don't know whether you ever got it. Nearly every day I go to see my cousin, the one who lives opposite your Grandmother Mina. How did you celebrate New Year's Eve? As I think you know already, we are in mourning for my 12 year old cousin who, as I told you before, was killed by a grenade. You knew her very well because we all used to play together when you came to Sarajevo.

So we couldn't celebrate New Year's Eve. The situation here is a bit quieter. It's not as bad as it was a few days ago.

How are you getting on at school? In Sarajevo no one goes to school and I have to admit that I miss it a little. I should love to see you but I don't believe I ever shall again. It's snowing here at the moment. The real winter is nearly here. People are cutting down trees all over the city so they can light fires to warm themselves and cook their food. I wonder when we shall go and eat cievapcici* together again. Or celebrate Bajram** by taking Kurban to the needy.

Amra***

*Cievapcici: Little rolls of minced meat served with chopped chives, raw onion and hot peppers.
**Bajram: a Moslem feast on which presents, called Kurban, are distributed to people in need.
***For more letters from the 14-year-old Amra to her best friend Laura, see pp. 131 and 145. See also the letter from Laura on p. 148.

Sarajevo, 7 January 1993

Dear Maca,

If ever this letter should get to you, it is to tell you not to worry about us. One way or another we are managing. Igor and Tano manage to bring us something to eat and the German marks that I had put by for a rainy day have helped somewhat even though black market goods are frighteningly expensive and no one knows if things are going to get even harder. We have managed to organize some heating even without electricity by adapting the stove to run on diesel fuel, and this – when we can get hold of it – comes straight out of the pipe. They say it's dangerous, but every moment here is dangerous, and when all's said and done we are only concerned with surviving the next few hours without too much cold and damp. It's −15° today. We are also frightened of getting hepatitis, typhoid, lice, scabies, etc. Such is life . . . I can remember the second world war, but that was nothing compared to this. My greatest worry is for Zoran. He has lost thirty kilos and goes in terror even of his own shadow, because here it is like Texas, you can be shot and no one will even notice. He stays put all day long and his only wish is to leave Sarajevo. Tano and I could probably leave with the help of the Jewish community, but if we did we could never return, because as soon as anyone goes away someone else moves into their home. So we have decided to stay whatever the consequences. All that matters to me is that Cole and Zoran should come out of this alive, especially Zoran who is in a dreadful state. Cole is working and has a very pretty girlfriend, a chemistry student.

My dear Maca, if you want to help us, put aside a few lira, because if we survive we shall be as poor as churchmice, hungry, thirsty, naked and barefoot. Every now and then Mira, Fule's daughter, comes to us to get warm and drink some broth thickened with flour, because they have no heating. They have already burnt the writing desk, the stools and even the piano on the stove. Two bombs fell on their apartment, so her parents went away and she was left all alone. We hear news of Cana every so often. She is living in a dreadful part of town, Pero Kosoric Square, where every single skyscraper has been burnt out. Pavla's flat has been demolished and she is being cared for by Ifeta. I don't want to weary you with all this, but there are so many things to tell you about.

Last Sunday I went to see Zoran, because he is frightened of coming to my place as it's more dangerous. I stayed with them for two or three hours and then we all went together to see a man who lives in a small house and has a stove on which he lets people cook. Ifeta prepared a meal for us all and then I set out for home. As soon as I had left, they began to shoot from Trebevic, at first with bullets, then with grenades. Just as I was passing the building where Cole lives, a grenade exploded only about 10 metres away. I tried to get into one of the buildings, but all the entrances were locked. In a fit of desperation I tried to break into one but it was no good. I began to run, faster and faster, and when I got to our own entrance I saw that a grenade had fallen on the police station. As soon as I got inside the door people came and gave me sugar and water to help me recover from the fright and the exhaustion. Yesterday, on my way to collect our humanitarian aid parcel I noticed that the last trees in the park had been cut down. Our beautiful park is now stripped bare.

Don't be worried by my mention of humanitarian aid. That is all that any of us has now, and everyone collects it, even ex-president Mikulic, and Kurtovic. Even Neno Jurin goes to Caritas because now we are all needy.

We all send our love, dearest Maca, and when we think of your good fortune in being away from here and not having to experience all this, it makes us feel better.

Everyone sends you their best wishes.

Yours, Nada

Staljingrad*, 11 January 1993

My adorable Jelusko,

At last I have in my hands your letter written on 3 December. It made record time – only 34 days. So now I know that you got some of the letters I sent to Vela Luka, though unfortunately not which of them. I don't know the dates on them but these, whatever they are, will tell you how long the letters were travelling around before they arrived. Many will undoubtedly have been lost, but some will still be on their way to you by routes known only to themselves. So far I have had only two letters from you and this latest one that Kalcioni left on the table here. This is because I am once more at the front line and hardly ever come home.

My one and only love, I feel I must ask your forgiveness for momentary lapses of faith, but you, on the other hand, must realize that I have been completely separated from you for months, for eight interminable months, with no way of communicating. I have sent dozens of letters without receiving any replies. So in my moments of depression I grabbed hold of pen and paper and expressed my every thought, even the least important, in my letters to you, with no attempt at embellishment. Today I ask your forgiveness. For today, you see, is the tenth birthday of our son Zenja, and I can't even give him a cuddle. This hurts dreadfully. There's nothing I can do about it except grit my teeth (or dentures, in my case) and try to struggle on.

After a few days of relative calm, this January 11th is being rent by explosions on every side. The whole city is shuddering, and a little while ago, at about a quarter past one, our building was hit by a grenade near the main entrance. It was an armour-plated shell designed to pierce concrete and luckily the hole is not large. I was sad to see children carrying away the casing, about 5 kilos of steel that would have made an interesting addition to my collection of lethal objects that fall from the sky. There will be such a lot to show Romanceros when we are all together again.

Oh how I miss you, Djile. I dreamt about you last night. We

---

*Ironic word-play on Stalingrad, the last city in recent history to suffer a prolonged siege, and a hypothetical 'Aljingrad', or 'city of Alija' (Izetbegovic), the Bosnian president.

were lying in each others' arms and you were warm and smelt of perfume. I often ponder my dreams and have even read some books about their meaning, arriving at the conclusion that most of mine represent a wish to run away from this inferno to an idealised place of safety. The strange thing is that I have absolutely no fear of dying. But I certainly do not want to be crippled and become a burden to other people. My dreams also show an awareness of the fact that I could be carried off at any moment. I remember your saying that I had a wild side to my nature. The war, and especially these months of fighting, have proved you right but with one difference: it is not a wild side but a bestial one. However, I have no intention of going into details that you might find intolerable, but I can assure you, and others would bear me out, that I am not an evil man.

Throughout the conflict my mind has been unhindered by emotions (hate, anger, etc.) and works like a machine. I take note of everything, my senses are razor-sharp, my reflexes good, my physical condition (despite malnutrition) ditto, I manage to concentrate and therefore to avoid making mistakes. Indeed, I cannot afford to make mistakes, they would be fatal: this is no game. Of course one has to rely on an element of luck, but I feel that you, my guardian angel, are always with me. After being wounded and cared for, I also realized that the men in my unit like and appreciate me; this was a most welcome discovery and I shall be terribly sorry to leave them, but I must because I fully intend to survive this crazy war and am trying to pull back into safer areas. Keep your fingers crossed.

I see from your letter that you are thinking of going to Austria. Don't be too hasty, lovey. Decisions like that, that change one's whole life, are extremely important and should only be taken together. Don't you agree? I know that life is difficult for you, more difficult than you could ever have dreamed in your worst nightmare, but you must realize, you must believe that all this is a terrible but ONLY TEMPORARY state of affairs, that came about without our consent and will end in the same way, and given good will on our side even the memory of it can be completely obliterated. You mustn't give up. I – in my rare free moments – dream of our future. I enjoy making plans for it. In my head I have already designed the house that we shall build one day on the shores of Lake Jablanica, Our House, a strange, pyramid-shaped, sunny house surrounded by lawns and trees. Try and do some sketches. I'm sure that for you, with your experience, such an idea would be a marvellous challenge.

I am going to have to cut down the trees in our garden if I am not to die of cold this winter. I shall hate doing it, but I have no choice.

Every time I go to rejoin my unit or come back home I have to cross the railway lines. You know what memories the station holds for us. Now, when I see it deserted, silent, dead, pock-marked by shrapnel and blackened by fire, and the skeletons of burnt-out carriages – the very same ones in which we travelled and beside which we used to meet, and embrace, and freeze – standing there, it makes me terribly sad. And every time I glance down the line towards the curve where your face disappeared from my sight, pressed against the window of the carriage, and I think of the day when it will reappear at the same point. And I live for that day.

I spent New Year's Eve with friends, and lean and gloomy it was too. But something happened to me at midnight. All of a sudden, a few seconds after midnight, my spirit left my body and flew to you. I am convinced, totally, that somewhere, half way between Sarajevo and Vela Luka, our astral bodies met and embraced. The feeling was so intense that even other people in the room noticed that something was happening to me. When the clock struck midnight we all stood up to greet the new year, myself included, and I stood there absolutely still, looking southwards through a bombproof window. After a couple of minutes I snapped out of it and returned to normal. A minute or two later Franjo came up to me and in a very strange voice quite unlike his usual one, asked me: 'Where have you been?'

When we had all finished exchanging our New Year greetings I came home, lay down on the bed and stayed there, wide awake, imagining you in every detail. And it was like being in a different world. Sarajevo is in the grip of the ice. On 7 January I found the whole flat frozen up. Even some tea in the kitchen was frozen solid. To my great distress, all the plants have become war-victims. Our cactus has died. It was in such poor condition that it will never recover. But you will see, that the day will come when we shall plant another. My love, I must say goodbye for now, I am going back to the mountains. Kiss Maja for me and give Romanceros a cuddle. Stay with him always, be sensible and patient. I embrace you.

Pavle

Sarajevo, 15 January 1993

Dear Zlatko, Gordana, Una and Jasna,

We were very glad to get your letter dated 28 December, because now we know where you are and that you are well. We have also received the parcel from France, which arrived at exactly the right moment because there was nothing left in the house apart from a little rice.

Zlatko, have you found a job? What are you living on? Are you managing?

All three of us are well. Mamma comes every morning for a cup of coffee before going to the shelter. She sleeps there with Kemo. It is very cold. The mountains around Sarajevo are covered with snow and there is no heating in the shelter, only concrete floor and walls. It is very damp. Mamma dresses very warmly, she wears her fur coat and even sleeps in it. I prefer to stay in the flat even though there is no power and no heating. It begins to get dark at four o'clock. There are no matches, candles or lighters, so all I can do is sit in the dark and at seven I go to bed. I cook and wash the clothes by hand, but we have been without water for days and the buckets we filled are empty. Only one pane of glass has survived the bombing, all the others are broken.

Josko died last week and Mirsad, Ferida's son, has had his right leg amputated. In Maglaj, Fudo, Enver and Haris have all been injured and Haris, who was wounded more severely than the others, is still in hospital. About Emir coming to you, it is not possible because he does not want to, and even if he did there is no way he could get out of Sarajevo.

Look after yourselves,
Grandfather

Sarajevo, 15 January 1993

Dear Laura,

As I haven't sent the letter yet, I thought I might as well add a couple of words. The situation in Sarajevo hasn't got any better at all, and now they've started to shoot a lot again. I don't go down to the cellar any more because the shooting has been so much lighter over the last few days. I hardly ever go out of the house except to go round to the neighbours from time to time, because I'm afraid of the grenades. Every so often I go to see my cousin who has had a baby called Nadia and who lives opposite your Granny Mina. Granny Mina is well. She showed me some photographs of you. I would be ever so happy if you could send me a photo of yourself. I shall try to send you one of me as soon as we can get it developed, but in Sarajevo, with no electricity, this is impossible for the moment. A few days ago we had a letter from my brother in Malesia. He went there to study because he won a scholarship. We are all very happy about this.

My parents are well and I hope yours are too. I love you very much and send you lots of affectionate good wishes.

Amra Foco

Sarajevo, 16 January 1993

My dear ones,

How are you? Where are you? How are you managing to live? I have no idea whether or not you received the letter I wrote replying to the one the five hundred pacifists took with them before the new year. I have heard that they may begin sorting the post in Sarajevo again, so I hope you will write to me more often. Grandad is delighted that his granddaughter is doing well at school, and always thinks of Jasna when he puts on his socks. Zlatko and Goco, what are you up to?

These are very difficult days for us. There has been no light for forty five days, and the water situation continues to deteriorate. Kemo manages to bring us a little every two or three days. To give you some idea of the situation, Miro has to walk from Visnjik to the brewery in Pivra to fetch water, a distance of five kilometres. Soon after the beginning of the year we began to have problems with the water pipes and the drains because they froze up. Kemo and I worked as a team for five days and managed to unblock them. On the twelfth of this month the balcony was set on fire. An incendiary device fell on top of a cardboard box full of plastic toys. We managed to put the blaze out, but I inhaled so much of the poisonous fumes that I was ill. Half an hour later a bullet shattered the light in Kemo's room and bullets even penetrated the kitchen. Had I not thrown myself to the floor I should have been killed.

There is no point in even thinking about leaving Sarajevo at the moment. It is impossible. If you have an opportunity to send us a parcel, and if you have enough money, please do so, because we have almost no food left.

My love to Iso, Azra, Aida, Maria and Renzo.

You must not say anything to the children about our difficulties.

Kiss them all for me.

Your very loving Papa

Sarajevo, 18 January 1993

Dear Pierre,

I don't know if this letter will ever get to you. Some journalists working for French television promised Hamo that they would take both my letters (one for you and one for my aunt) to Paris. In Sarajevo it is now very cold, there is no power and the entire city has been without water for three days, so it is very wearying to queue up every day in the cold. But then, if you are very, very lucky, you can fill your container with water and carry it home. Still, we are used to coping with such problems. Indeed, our whole day is reduced to coping with mundane problems that you and other normal people don't even have to think about. On top of which, the shooting and killing goes on. Do you remember the park near our place where we used to go for walks? There are no trees there any more and it has become one big graveyard. They bury nearly all the young people from between nineteen and twenty nine years old in it, and there are friends, acquaintances, fellow students. A very good friend of mine, Almir, has died. And Ramo whom you met when you were here. The Sarajevo you knew last summer no longer exists. Nearly all the tall buildings have been burnt or reduced to rubble. Even that wonderful building, the National Library, that you wanted to photograph. We went there while it was burning and made a human chain to try to save a few of the books, and I cried at the sight of Sarajevo's best library going up in flames. But I have seen so much death and destruction over the last ten months that nothing surprises me any more. It is very difficult to describe all that has happened and that is still happening. And if it is difficult for me, who have seen it with my own eyes, imagine how difficult it must be for anyone far away to believe that cruelty on such a scale is really going on. To think that the beings we used to call 'human', people we actually knew, that we met in the street, could have generated such destruction. Sometimes I close my eyes and try to imagine something of beauty; in such moments I recall Paris and the times we spent together. And I wonder if I shall ever see Paris again, if you and I will ever laugh again over silly little things as we did in that bar in Montparnasse. I have not yet lost all hope that this horror will end and life return to normal. But I am afraid that none of us who have lived through this experience here will ever be able to see things in the same light as the rest of the world. There is so much more I could tell you about the bombing, the fear, the longing to see people you know and not being able to because it is now impossible even to move from one part of Sarajevo to another, but I would need much more time. Perhaps the time will come, and I hope so much that it does, when we shall meet again and be together and then we shall be able to talk. Perhaps this madness will end. I think you know that it is impossible to get out of Sarajevo, but if you could let us have a letter of authorization it would be worth a try. You could try to get it to us via the Franco-Bosnian Association or the Adventist Church. I forgot to tell you that I managed to sit the third-year exams. The university is closed because of sniper fire in the area, but they managed to move the course to another part of the city, close to where I live. So whenever I hear that the firing has died down somewhat, I try to get there. I shouldn't want you to think that everything in Sarajevo is dreadful and that we have lost all hope. There is still life here and those of us who remain try to keep well and to behave normally. I have had good experiences too in this war. I have met some wonderful people and some have become personal friends. Some of my former friends I never want to see again. My head buzzes with a million thoughts every day; sometimes I believe one thing, and sometimes another. But the day must come when it will all be over, and I hope that we emerge victorious. Give my regards to all in Paris. I love you very, very much and I am thinking of you.

Tanja

Sarajevo, 21 January 1993

Dear Ana,

Sarajevo is no more! At least not your Sarajevo, our Sarajevo, the beautiful city. There's not even any water. There is now a new dimension to our misery: dirt and thirst.

You, my darling, must begin a new life, away from the Balkans. I, on the other hand, shall die here as an idealist. I believe in you and in your abilities, and I know that you will find a way to live life honestly. Don't come back while you have the chance of staying where you are. The power is off yet again, people can't cook so they have to go looking for firewood. I remember how you used to complain of the smog blackening the trees in front of your school. The smog has disappeared because not a single factory is working and there are no cars. But the trees have also disappeared, down to the last branch. Birds, with no branches to perch on, die of exhaustion and starvation. The dogs are all dying. Beautiful, highly bred dogs roam the streets hungry and abandoned. Their owners may be dead, but anyway people do not have enough food for themselves, let alone for animals! One kilo of potatoes costs 25 German marks, a litre of oil costs 20.

Thank God we are in good health so we can cope with all this.

I think of you all the time and send you my love,

Papa

Sarajevo, 22 January 1993

My darlings,

Mevla has told me (you remember the blonde lady over the road who was always tending her garden?) that an Italian who lives in Florence has arrived to marry a girl from Sarajevo, and that they will soon be going home and could take a letter with them. I immediately sat myself down by the light to write to you. I make a point of saying 'by the light' because the people in the block opposite ours have had their power reconnected, while we have been without since 7 December, and we have connected our system to their supply by wires running across the grass. They managed to get themselves designated a 'priority case', so every time the hospitals get some electricity, so do they. They have allowed us to connect the wires. So now, after such a long time, we have a light bulb in our former bedroom, a little electric fire and even television. Today, for the first time since the outbreak of the war, we had baked potatoes! What a joy . . .

We heard how very concerned you were after a radio report saying that a bomb had fallen in our street. In actual fact it fell on the street next to this. I often think that you worry more about us than we do ourselves. We are now on the waiting list for a telephone call. Once again there is a number one can ring to book a call, like there was last November. Only this time there is such a to-do! First you have to go to the post office and pay in advance, then you have to dial the booking number from home hundreds and hundreds of times before getting through. There is only a single line for the whole of Sarajevo. We are now waiting and hoping that we shall be able to phone you sooner or later, because our friend Nesmin knows someone at the post office who could 'pull some strings' for us. You see what we have to do, my darlings, just to secure a tiny bit of normal life. And yet it is amazing how people always seem to manage! Today the water came on again after forty two days! This is undoubtedly the biggest relief. I always used to maintain that electricity was more important than water. It is not. Now I am aware that it is not . . . The cold, the dreadful −15°, is over, fortunately. I hope it will not return, though there are many who fear the contrary because, as they say, there's still a long winter ahead. We have no great hopes of the spring, unable to believe that our suffering will begin to diminish. We all pray God that the bombing will stop. One could at least get out of the house and then everything would be easier.

Will Geneva do any good? I doubt it, because in Pale they are all consummate liars and nothing has been done about the famous artillery hand-over since the beginning of the war. Because were it to happen – and the mad psychiatrist* has said so quite clearly – the Bosnian army would be the strongest of the lot.

All I know is that this has gone on too long and we are all weary and need peace and the simple things of life. If only you could imagine how we dream about walking down the road, any road, even down a bare, treeless avenue strewn with rubble and broken glass, that wouldn't matter. It would be enough to be able to walk normally, without the fear of shells forcing you to scurry from one side to the other.

Will normal days ever come back?

There are times when I am sure they will, others when I'm not. Papa goes to work every day. You know what he's like, he's managed to get a lot 'cracking' and certainly has a lot of work.

Just as well. And where he works everyone is now on the same level and no one talks about status any more. Even I was able to get to the television centre yesterday for the first time in two months. My heart was in my mouth. The place is freezing now and everyone working there is frozen stiff, the rooms are deserted and their windows all broken. The only part of it that has any semblance of normality is the underground bunker, from where they are still managing to broadcast. All the rest is horrendous. Darling, your little sister, our 'housemaid par excellence' and our main procurer of bread and water, is managing. She too, in this war, has 'attended' a new and cruel school. And graduated with flying colours! No trace remains of the vulnerable little girl she used to be. She is now prepared to cope even with the most difficult problems. I wish she had not been forced to learn these skills, but at the same time I am proud of the fact that she has shown much more strength than I would ever have thought possible. The fact that she has managed to maintain her normal weight proves this . . .

Pretty ones, if you only knew how often we think of you!

*Slobodan Karadzic, a psychiatrist by profession.

Especially at that time of day, my son, when you get home from work. We 'see' the little one running to the door, Sanja has a meal ready, you take off your tie . . .

It's all so familiar, close but at the same time far away. I implore you to take some photographs and send them to us; you can't think how much we need them.

All the relatives are well. The Cerics have put a fire in the kitchen and spend whole days there. Aunt Hasna is coping, and although she has lost more weight than any of us, she still finds the energy to joke about it. Slobodan and Verica come round every Sunday and they cheer us up every time. He is working very hard and she goes every day to teach at the makeshift Faculty at the Law Courts. She complains about there being no students in the freezing courtrooms with their shattered windows. Well I never, the television announcer has just told us that our troops have taken Lapisnica. That's the hill from which the very first grenades were launched at us on that far distant 20 April! Good luck to them! Kiss the little one's blue eyes for me. Has he grown very much?

All our love,
Mamma

P.S. Strange things have happened in this war. Despite all this cold, there are no illnesses around. Not one of us has had a cold or been unwell. Even without food, people have managed to summon up their strength and become resistant.

We are all healthy, luckily.

Sarajevo, 7 February 1993

Dear Alen,

The journalist brought your letter. You can imagine our surprise. We also received the fax that you sent via Fedja. We're happy to know that you are well and in a job. I can't resist telling you that Mamma kisses your letter at least ten times a day and keeps it in front of her all the time.

We are all well, so far all safe and sound, and you needn't worry. We hope that this will all be over very soon and that the worst is now past.

It's not as cold as it was, perhaps the cold will not return and those who are up in the mountains around us will have to quit sooner or later whether they like it or not.

Dear Alen, don't send any parcels for now, we are managing quite well. We should prefer you to send us, if you can, another fax via Fedja.

We love you so much, we embrace you and are proud of you.

Mamma, Dado and Papa

Sarajevo, 9 February 1993

Dear Eci,

Your parcel of clothes was delivered by Toni. Luckily, as I no longer had any clothes to wear. I was having to borrow from neighbours and then return them. Two weeks ago clothes were very nearly the death of me. Ever since the war broke out, I have only left the house when it was absolutely necessary. But I had heard that Caritas were going to distribute clothes to refugees that Saturday, so I went along with a friend of mine, a refugee from Dobrinja. However, the distribution was cancelled so we came home early and minutes afterwards there was a massacre in Vase Miskin street. It was a miracle that we were not involved. Since then it hasn't even occurred to me to go out to look for clothes. Then your pack arrived, full of the most wonderful things. You can imagine how much thinner I am when I tell you that I fitted into your green jeans. All the neighbours come round to my place to see 'something pretty'. Thank you, thank you a thousand times, and may health and happiness be yours.

Toni is standing over me waiting to take this letter, but I don't know how to end it. Believe me, I no longer have the strength to do anything, not even to write a letter. I hope you can understand. You have no idea of the state of mind of the people here. We try desperately hard to stay normal, but circumstances are getting worse. Bijafra came to see me the other day, and even he seemed mad. He told me that he hadn't slept for three months and attends the neuropsychology clinic at the hospital. I never dreamed it could come to this. Sarajevo is a city of the dead, the crippled and the insane. And this is all the future holds for us.

We continually discuss ways of leaving Sarajevo. Your mother is hoping for a place in one of the convoys for the sick and the old. Despite, and in the middle of all this madness, my Djenana has married Slavisa, after living with him for a hundred years. So many people are getting married, and others are separating.

Dear Eci, I can't describe what is happening here. When someone comes to see me I find I have nothing left to say. I met Zlatan Skenderovic a few months ago. He is also mad. He was talking nonsense. I keep remembering his words when I asked him 'Tunjo, when will it all end?' and he said coldly: 'When they kill us all.'

We live, as it were, in a cage. Every day is the same. I have got used to everything, to being hungry, dirty, thirsty, but the worst thing of all is that I have lost heart.

I live in the ruins of my apartment. Nothing else matters any more.

My dear Eci, pray for us here. I hope I haven't wearied you too much with my ravings. If you can, if someone else returns to Sarajevo, as I expect they will because this war is going to last a long time, send me another letter. Greetings from the besieged city,

Marjana

Sarajevo, 9 February 1993

Dear Grandad,

We got the letter you wrote in December and we are replying immediately. We are all well. Sanja and I are being good. In your letter you say that you gathered that Mummy doesn't work any more because the war doesn't allow her to. But that's not the reason. The reason is that the building where her offices were has been completely burnt out. Sarajevo, you know, is not what it used to be. Bombs fall on the city every day, so we cannot use the room where we always used to play.

We eat the food that the world sends us: lunch packets that are 10 or 15 years old and full of preservatives.

We got one parcel, but we don't know who sent it. Granny got one just like it. The label on the parcel only says: 'Alsace Sarajevo'. You say in your letter that Jasmina is doing well in school, but that her marks are really her mother's marks because she is doing her homework. You should tell Jasmina that she must do her own homework, because you know the saying: 'A little work, a little play, to keep us going – and so, good-day!'

No one goes to school any more here, but there are teachers who go into people's houses and give lessons.

Sanja has learnt to read and write. Papa conducts concerts for the soldiers and teaches them wartime songs.

Sanja and I have formed a little group with some friends and we put on shows for the other tenants in the building. We did one on New Year's Eve. Dear Grandad, you say that you have found many old friends in Rovigno and I am very happy for you.

Right now they are starting to shell us again and I must close this letter quickly because we have to fly down to the cellar.

We love you very much, take care,

Maja and Sanja

Sarajevo, 11 February 1993

My dearest, adored daughters,

I am trying to find the strength to write to you even though today
– as, indeed throughout these last few weeks – I feel totally, utterly
drained. And that is not difficult to explain since I have wasted
away physically until there is almost nothing of me left. We have
learnt from your friends that you two are well, and that is all
that matters to us. Your mother, however, like all mothers, is
not satisfied with that, and would like to hear it from your
own lips. I enclose a drawing of the part of the flat in which
we live now, since it is impossible to heat the other rooms.
These last few days haven't been so bad, the temperature is
only 5 degrees below freezing whereas in January it fell to
minus 15 and minus 18 and we thought we were going mad.
We never undressed, and stayed wrapped up in blankets day
and night. Then one day my finger started hurting. It was
swollen and kept getting worse. Then it developed a lesion.
Your mother kept saying: 'We must try to be strong for our
daughters' sake; we must try to survive so that we can see them
again; please try to be strong.' But I told her: 'Don't worry, they're
big girls now.'
  Not one of your letters has ever got to us. We're curious, we want
to know everything: your heart-throbs, your hair-styles, whether
you have got fatter or thinner (please look after yourselves and
stay beautiful).
  Bessy is fine; your mother says she wouldn't know what to do
without her and Bessy herself has an almost pathological attach-
ment to your mother. I am slightly jealous. But don't worry, I'm
fit, I'm still alive and only worried about this finger that refuses to
heal. I have also started to limp, not that that affects me too greatly
as my appearance is no longer as important to me as it was before
the war. You know the importance I attached to being always neat
and well dressed, but one can't do that any longer. Survival is all
that matters.
  But nothing that can happen to us will ever undo the fact that
we have been a wonderful, and united, family. Life has given us 26
years filled with beautiful things, and some sad ones, and in these
hard times it is terribly important to remember that. The story of

our family will always be a matter of record, and even the future is already predetermined.

Here we have been stripped of everything, but the one thing that no one can take from me is the right to go on loving you however and however much I want to.

I think of you always and embrace you.

Your father

Sarajevo, 13 February 1993

Dear Papa and dear everyone else,

This is our happiest day ever because at last, after ten months, we were able to hear your voices on the phone. We're so happy to hear you are well, especially you, Papa.

We're all fine, it's not so cold now and we're hoping the power may return, too. We managed to find some firewood to keep us warm. I was able to organize the call with the help of a colleague who works at the office of telephone communications.

Mamma was delighted that you were all at home so that she could speak to all of you. Dear Papa, how do you spend your days as a refugee? I went to collect your pension today and immediately bought some German marks because dinars are now useless. Don't worry about us, as you see, we are managing reasonably well. That's all that matters at the moment.

We love you all very much and send you hugs and kisses,

Fika, Seka, Jasna, Maja and Sanja

Sarajevo, 13 February 1993

Dear Laura,

Even though I can't be sure that my letter will ever get to you, I still had to write. I have already written to you twice before, but don't know if you got the letters. They say that deliveries of mail may be possible, so you could try writing to me. Every day I hope for a letter from you, but I have never received one. We're all fine. The heavy shelling has started up again here. Luckily, not near here. People continue to die. It's horrible!

I get terribly bored. I never want to do anything. Every now and then I read some stupid book. There's no electricity, and water only occasionally.

I often see your Granny Mina. I went to see her on your birthday and we talked a lot about you. She is very well. Yesterday, because it was her birthday, I went to see Delila, and she sends you her love . . .

Do you remember the nursery school at the bottom of our road? There's nothing left of it, it has been completely flattened.

How do you like your school? Did you choose the one for 'Tourism' or the language school? Give my regards to your family and write if you can. I send you my love and a big, big hug,

Amra
HAPPY BIRTHDAY!

Sarajevo, 18 February 1993

Dear Azra,

I am writing to you again although I have never received any replies from you. Dear Azra, I also wrote a letter to you which I sent to one of your friends in Kraljebo, but I don't know whether he managed to call you and read it to you over the phone. I keep thinking about you and your family and should welcome some news. How are you, and how is life? How is Laura? I often go to see your mother. I find her well considering the situation here where no one is well. I learned from her that you saw Haris in Geneva during the demonstration. I am reasonably well. My sister has been living with me since the death of her son.

The cold is too great for comfort.

Shells are raining down every day and people are being killed both out in the streets and indoors. The city has a ghostly look about it; you could mistake it for Vukobar.

Azra, sadly I have a piece of really dreadful news that I must communicate to you. Yesterday, on the 17th February, Amra, your Laura's friend, was killed by one of four grenades that hit their apartment. When I heard about it, I couldn't stop crying all day. Such terrible things are happening here that maybe even we ourselves, if we survive, will never know about them. Amra will be buried tomorrow, 19 February, at Vrbanjusa, near the grave of her grandfather who died two months ago.

When you receive my letter, try to overlook my shaky handwriting. It expresses my state of mind at this time. I can't for the moment think of anything to add, since there's nothing nice to write about but only news of the dreadful things that are happening. I send you my very best wishes and await your news with great anxiety.

Nuna

Sarajevo, 19 February 1993

My darling daughters,

I am completely drained. I had to tell you. My veins have been drained, and my arteries, kidneys, brain, heart. Everything; but what frightens me most is that my soul is now completely drained.

I'm sorry, but I have to tell you cruel things now, tell you about the friends I have lost, who have been killed: the painter Rizovic, Cindric, Zoran Bajbutovic, Vesna Bugarski, Alija Kucukalic (he a while ago).

And then there are all those who are alive, but only half alive.

They tell me that I must live, and I listen to them, but I cannot do it.

My loves, my little ones, forgive me. Don't be angry with your papa because he has become so EMPTY. Completely EMPTY.

I feel like an actor with no audience.

. . . We thought we could fly
But we fell to the ground instead.
All of a sudden
Everything exploded around us.

However, there is one thing that I must tell you, that I love you very, very much and the only thing around me that does not make me unhappy is the knowledge that you two, your mother and poor Bessy are alive.

With much love,
your Papa*

*Nikola Nescovic, the day before his death.

from Milan to Sarajevo, 22 February 1993

My dear Amra,

This is Laura! How are you? I am well, but this stupid war looks as if it will never end and makes me very afraid for all of you. Thank you for your birthday wishes. I have not received any other letters from you, they may have been lost somewhere in Yugoslavia or in Italy, I have no idea. I am so sad that we cannot see each other for so long. I miss you all, but you especially. I miss Sarajevo, Bascarsija, the river Miljacka, cievapcici and lots of other things.

I'm not doing very well at school because I can't concentrate, I keep thinking about the war. I do like the school I've chosen, however. I'm learning three languages, English, French and German. I've found a boy I like, too. His name is Gianluca.

Do you see anything of Alica and Alma? Please give them my love and tell them I miss them too. I wonder sometimes how come you're not afraid to leave the cellar in this terrible situation. I'm sure that if I were in your place I'd never be able to move. How are your mother and father? Please give them my regards. And the dog? Does he get frightened of the war too? I'm sure he does. I'm enclosing a photo with this letter. But it's not a good one of me. My goodness, I look a fright! I send you lots and lots of good wishes and much love. Don't ever forget me.

Laura

On 17 February Amra Foco was killed by flying fragments – under her parents' eyes – when their apartment in Dimitrija Tucodica Street was hit by a shell. She was fourteen and a half years old.

Her friend Laura wrote in her diary: 'Today, 16 March 1993, is the worst day of my life, because I have learned that my friend Amra is dead, killed by a grenade. Amra, you have always been my best friend and you always will be. I shall never forget you. Laura.'

AND THE SIEGE
WENT ON . . .

Peace Conference Chronology

24 June 1992, New York
In the National Assembly the association 'Démocrates Sans Frontières' calls for a conference on Peace and Democracy in the former Yugoslavia.

29 June 1992, Paris
The French President, François Mitterand, proposes an international conference on Bosnia-Hercegovina.

August 1992, New York
The United Nations Security Council approves Amendment No. 760 by which UN forces in Bosnia are authorized to use 'all measures that may be necessary' in pursuance of the transport and distribution of humanitarian aid 'to Sarajevo and wherever aid may be required'.

24 August 1992, London
Preliminary discussions on a Peace Conference on Bosnia-Hercegovina are initiated in London.

27 August 1992, London
Hosted by the British Prime Minister, John Major, the London Peace Conference opens. Forty delegations or 'interested parties' and 450 delegates take part. Under the joint leadership of the UN Secretary General, Dr Boutros-Ghali, John Major (current President of the EC) and the American Secretary of State Lawrence Eagleburger, the Conference agrees on the following points:

1. A commitment not to use force to resolve the Bosnian conflict.
2. The immediate closure of all detention camps.

3. Respect for human rights.
4. Guaranteed integrity of existing frontiers within the former Federation and the commitment that 'Ethnic Cleansing' procedures should not be used to modify them.

It is also decided that David Owen, founder of the Social Democrat Party and a former British Foreign Minister, should replace Lord Carrington as EC mediator.

The international community expresses its condemnation of Serbia as the aggressor and proposes an embargo to include armaments.

October 1992, London
The Peace Conference on the former Yugoslavia continues throughout the autumn. No overall agreement is reached, but the outlines of what will eventually be known as the 'Vance-Owen Plan' begin to take shape.

The decision is taken to convene a new Peace Conference in Geneva.

2 January 1993, Geneva
Representatives of the three warring factions arrive in Geneva. These are: Radovan Karadzic speaking for the Serbs, Mate Boban for the Croats, and the Bosnian President Izetbegovic for the Moslems. The mediators, Cyrus Vance (acting for the UN) and Lord Owen (acting for the EC), put forward a plan which can be summarized as follows:

1. The division of Bosnia-Hercegovina into ten provinces.
2. These provinces would be denied international judicial status.
3. The three major ethnic groups would be recognized as constituent parts of the state of Bosnia-Hercegovina.
4. Every problem relating to the three ethnic groups would be referred to a central constituent assembly and every constitutional amendment would have to be agreed by all three ethnic groups.
5. Both the provinces and the central government would be provided with a democratic parliament elected by an executive also democratically elected.

6. Bosnia-Hercegovina would be progressively de-militarized.

3 January 1993, Washington
The Secretary of State Lawrence Eagleburger expresses his sense of outrage at the crimes committed against the Moslems and proposes the setting up of a war tribunal. The Pentagon presents a plan drawn up with the help of General Colin Powell and Major John Shalikashvili, commander-in-chief of NATO. Briefly, the five points of the plan are as follows:

1. To institute No-Fly Zones. A reinforcement of measures proposed in the October resolution.
2. To expand the Relief Operation. The US undertakes to increase its present number of 23,000 men in the Croatian ports and providing escorts for aid convoys to Sarajevo.
3. To arm the Bosnians. The US will request the Security Council to raise the embargo on war materials to Bosnia.
4. To protect Kosevo and Macedonia. The US proposes to send troops to Albania and Kosevo.
5. To create Safe Havens. To guarantee the security of these, the US would be prepared to send in additional land forces.

6 January 1993, Geneva
All negotiations are suspended for the Orthodox Christmas.

8–12 January 1993, Geneva
The UN Security Council announces that it has accepted the Vance-Owen Plan. The negotiations are resumed and continue throughout the whole month of January without the three factions reaching an agreement.

11 March 1993, Paris
At the invitation of President Mitterand, the Serbian President Slobodan Milosevic agrees to a meeting with the two peace negotiators, Cyrus Vance and David Owen.

21 March 1993, Belgrade
General Philippe Morillon travels to Belgrade on a mission to persuade the Serbian President, Milosevic, to accept the Vance-Owen Plan on behalf of the Bosnian Serbs.

2 May 1993, Athens
The Greek Prime Minister Constantine Mitsotakis hosts a conference at which the Serbian President Milosevic, the Yugoslavian president Cosic and the president of the self-styled Republic of Pale, Radovan Karadzic, all take part.

Karadzic signs an agreement that provides for a 10 km corridor in the north of Bosnia linking Serb territories.

5 May 1993, Pale
The parliament at Pale refuses to ratify the plan accepted in Athens.

22 May 1993, Washington
The ministers for foreign affairs from the US, Russia, France, Great Britain and Spain sign a 'Programme of concerted action' for Bosnia. Six 'safe havens' to be created around the cities of Tuzla, Bihac, Srebrenica, Sarajevo, Goradze and Zepa, under the guaranteed protection of the UN.

The Moslems comment is: 'They want to put us in Indian reservations.'

The plan drawn up in Washington by the five ministers for foreign affairs definitively buries the Vance-Owen Plan. Thorvold Stoltenberg takes over from Cyrus Vance.

5 June 1993, Geneva
To decide on the division of the new borders of the three nations, the Serb President Milosevic, the Croat President Tudjman and seven members of the Bosnian Presidency meet for a plenary session in Geneva. They discuss the division of Bosnia on ethnic lines into three states and consider maps and corridors.

6 June 1993, Geneva
Tudjman and Milosevic abandon the Geneva talks, but the members of the Bosnian Presidency (two Croats, two Moslems, two Serbs and one Yugoslav) continue discussions with the mediators Owen and Stoltenberg.

30 July 1993, Washington
The US and France give the Serb forces an ultimatum: the fighting ceases immediately or UN Resolution 836 will come into force, authorizing air attacks on the Serb positions.

7 August 1993, Brussels
The decision of NATO on how and when to commence the military attacks on Bosnia is awaited.

9 August 1993, Geneva
While waiting for a decision from Brussels, the Geneva Peace Talks are resumed. The main points under discussion are geographical. They are:

1. SARAJEVO. The Serbs propose a division of the city. The Moslems refuse, asking instead for 'free city' status.
2. The SAVA RIVER. The Moslems request access to the Sava-Dunav tidal basin. The Serbs refuse because the Sava River runs alongside the 'corridor' linking the Serbian communities of East and West.
3. PROTECTED AREAS. How to arrange a link between the Moslem enclaves in the East and others elsewhere.
4. ACCESS TO THE SEA. The Moslems insist on two outlets to the Adriatic, one at Ploce in Dalmatia and the other at Rijeka.

17 August 1993, Geneva
After a ten-day break, the talks are resumed. The three conflicting groups, Serbs, Croats and Moslems, agree that Sarajevo should

be put under the control of the UN. The Bosnian capital will be an 'open city', completely de-militarized except for UN troops. The plan is backed by a tripartite committee which is also to determine the borders of the 'nine municipalities' into which the urban territory is to be divided.

21 August 1993, Geneva

To break the deadlock created by the two issues of access to the River Sava and to the sea, Lord Owen and Thorvold Stoltenberg make two proposals:

1. River Sava: The mainly Moslem city of Brcko would be reached by a road and a railway, both protected, which would cross Serb territory by means of a projected fly-over.
2. Access to the sea: No coastal territory would be ceded to the Moslems but they would have internationally guaranteed access to the port of Ploce on the Adriatic seabord within Croat territory.

The mediators comment: 'We could do no more . . .'
The Moslems declare their DISSATISFACTION.
The Bosnian President, Izetbegovic, refuses to talk to journalists. He decides to visit New York and Washington before returning to Sarajevo.

The leaders of the three warring factions agree to return to Geneva on 30 August. In the meantime, a cease-fire is declared.

30 August 1993, Sarajevo

A special session of the predominently Moslem Bosnian parliament authorizes President Izetbegovic to reply to the Geneva peace proposals on behalf of the Assembly.

His reply will be: YES to signing the peace declaration but NO to the conditions considered unacceptable.

1 September 1993, Geneva

Alija Izetbegovic and Radovan Karadzic sign a preliminary compromise in five parts.

2 September 1993, Geneva
The Croatian President, Franjo Tudjman, unexpectedly leaves the UN headquarters, declaring: 'The negotiations have broken down . . . We will not accept the Moslem demands . . . I am returning to Zagreb.'

Besides the two mediators Owen and Stoltenberg, these talks were also attended by President Milosevic of Serbia, President Izetbegovic of Bosnia, the Secretary General of the United Nations Dr Boutros-Ghali, Charles Redman as the special envoy of the President of the US, and the Russian Foreign Minister Andrej Kozyrev.

Stoltenberg informs the press that the nub of the disagreement on this occasion was the Croats' refusal to hand over the port of Neum to the Moslems as a means of access to the sea.

The UN calls for an enquiry after the discovery of 98 mass graves in the zones currently engaged in warfare.

Shultz and Thatcher call on President Clinton to 'bomb immediately'.

15 September 1993, Geneva
Presidents Franjo Tudjman of Croatia and Alija Izetbegovic of Bosnia agree to a truce based on the following:

1. Complete cessation of hostilities in central Bosnia between Croats and Moslems before Saturday 18 September 1993.
2. Exchange of all prisoners.
3. An undertaking on both sides to allow free passage to UN aid convoys.
4. The setting up of a working party to discuss the formation of a New Bosnian Union comprising three ethnically-defined mini-republics: Serbian, Croatian and Moslem.

17 September 1993, Geneva
A further meeting between the three warring factions (Moslem, Serb and Croat) is planned for 23 September 1993 at Sarajevo airport. Those to take part besides President Izetbegovic of Bosnia are the Croatian President Franjo Tudjman, the leader of the 'Bosnian-Serb Parliament' Momcilo Krajisnik representing

Radovan Karadzic and the Serbian President Slobodan Milosevic, and the President of Montenegro, Momir Bulatovic.

30 September 1993, Sarajevo
President Izetbegovic of Bosnia rejects the Geneva Conference Peace Plan as unacceptable.

Karadzic, the leader of the self-styled Bosnian-Serb Republic, speaking from Pale, threatens reprisals and the overturning of territorial concessions made to the Bosnians . . .

Spring and Summer 1993

Sarajevo, 7 May 1993

Buenas dias, linda señora!
Quetal guapa? Yo soy bien, mucho bien. Encantado!
Good morning, my darling,

These greetings show you that I have been learning Spanish for two weeks now. There are five in the class but there's a big problem as we have no books. So I write down everything we're taught and compile a kind of language course at home. I don't know how much I'll be able to learn, but I am trying to do something useful.

Quite honestly, camp life is not much fun, and the only moments that pass pleasantly are those devoted to agriculture on the balcony. I have been admiring the plants I sowed since six o'clock this morning. They're growing. I know each one of them. The other day I went up to the attic and brought down – forgive the indelicacy – a sackful of pigeon poo, the perfect fertilizer. So you can be sure that the food we produce will be healthily free of all unnatural substances.

You remember that cupboard in the utility room? I emptied it, sowed onions, lettuces, carrots and celery in it and put it by the door, on the right. On the left I've put the wooden tub that miraculously did not end up in the stove last year. In it I've sown garlic, herbs and radishes. I fantasize about growing beans, potatoes, peas and tomatoes and supplying my vitamin needs with my own produce. I only hope the balcony won't collapse under the weight. I wish you were here to see it. Our neighbours' balconies are also full of vegetables. What can you expect, we're all trying to survive. A bunch of nettles on the black market costs five marks, and then it depends, they can cost more if they were grown over a latrine, less if grown underneath it. I wouldn't pay those leeches a single pfennig even if I were a millionaire.

May has begun with thunderstorms in the afternoon. The city is beginning to look green even though all the trees, sadly, were cut down last winter, but weeds and shrubs are sprouting everywhere. Wherever you look you see rubble, piles of rubbish and weeds. People climb over the rubble moving in a strange, uncoordinated way, with unseeing eyes, and the number of cripples and soldiers is always rising. Everything is dark and dismal. I keep hoping that one day it will be nothing but a bad memory. I have a feeling that things will calm down because the rest of the world has had enough of our bloody goings-on.

At times I imagine what I would be doing if there were no war. It's the weekend, and we would probably have been together by the lake, fishing perhaps, or going to Studenak Rock. Do you remember the day you brought wine and glasses? If only you knew how I loved your every movement and how I miss seeing you.

Yesterday I went up to the attic looking for containers for my agriculture. I found a folder of my painting attempts made between 1974 and 1978. They are very sweet memories. Even though I have so little time, I have the urge to paint again. Unfortunately, however, I have no paper, paints or brushes. Of all the things I would need I have only the good intentions.

This morning I spent a long time looking at your photograph over the bed. Then I took it down and put it in my wallet so that it will be with me up in the mountains, like your black hair-ribbon.

I am dreaming, my love, dreaming about us and our future. Beautiful dreams of love. I can't express how much I miss you, but in my thoughts you are always with me. Everything I do or think of doing I first discuss with you and ask your opinion and advice. Put simply, even though we are physically separated I am still in continuous contact with you. Oh! How I could hug you! I depend upon you, and without you I am like a drug addict who can't get a fix!

The other day I was reading Churchill's Memoirs of the Second World War and came across some lines by a poet whose name I have forgotten, and I make you a present of his words because I liked them so much:

Ye Gods! annihilate but space and time,
*And make two lovers happy!**

These words encapsulate perfectly the 'prayers' I mutter under my breath thinking of you and Romanceros.

Today is already 12 May, and this letter – started on the 7th – is becoming a little diary. I expect you have already noticed

*Alexander Pope, *Martinus Scriblerus*, 1727.

that as soon as I finish writing you one letter I immediately put another sheet of paper in the typewriter to start the next. This continuity, my adored one, represents the communication that binds me to you.

Yesterday I had a rather unpleasant job to do. A man came to our Jewish community worried about a cousin of his, an old lady, whom he had not seen for several days. I went with him to Vase Miskin Street, which is no longer called 'the street of Dignity' but 'the street of Shame', and we forced the door to her flat. The little old lady was in a coma and the flat was piled with rubbish. We took her to the hospital but since every hospital is chock-a-block and there was no hope of saving the old lady, we had to carry her home again. We left her with some cousins who live just opposite her hovel, but I doubt if she will last more than three or four days.

I have seen so many dreadful things since this war started and I do wonder how many more the city is concealing.

My so greatly loved one, I am at the end of this sheet and I must close the letter. Write to me, because I live giving thanks for your letters. I love you, my darling,

Pavle

Sarajevo, 2 June 1993

My darlings,

A torrent of feelings, the desire to be with you, to hug you, to kiss you, the need to cry with you in order to release in tears everything that has accumulated in my heart over this miserable year, is getting in the way of my starting this letter to you.

My mind is racing, my hand shaking, I can't write properly. I hope you will be able to read it all the same.

I should like to be able to express myself without exaggeration, but I can no longer find the dividing line between exaggeration and simple truth.

We're safe and well. Every day starts in the same way: I'm the first up, I run to get in the queue for bread, then for water, then go to the market to see what food I can get. Life is easier at the moment as it's warm and we do get occasional supplies of electricity and water. The shooting has died down somewhat, too, but the snipers make up for the lull every now and then, telling us: 'Don't forget about us! We're here!'

We are now disfigured, deformed; we have a fear of silence, of the ghostly hush that makes our hair stand on end more than the sound of shots and explosions.

Things have been slightly better, relatively speaking, for the past few weeks, but the winter was terrible.

We were luckier than some, because we had an ancient stove. Masses of people were unable to even heat up a cup of tea. The nights seemed to last for ever; we had to light the oil lamp as early as four o'clock in the afternoon. Not a candle to be had. But there were some who didn't even have an oil lamp and so endured darkness, hours and hours of darkness. Inside all was cold and dark, outside there was complete silence, fear, insecurity, terror.

Now with the return of the warm weather and longer days, all this is behind us, hopefully. There could never be another winter like that.

We have made many new friends, and have never spent so much time with our neighbours. We and the Ivecovic's are just like one big family. We do our cooking together and collect our firewood together. Their flat has been hit and those two lovely rooms on the side facing the hills have gone. Luckily, although they were all at home when it happened, no one was hurt.

So many people have lost all they had, and we try to help them whenever we can.

More and more people are coming to pay us visits. Many of them come to speak to Papa, to ask his advice or just thank him for having stayed on. As you know, he has constantly refused to go away, to abandon Sarajevo.

Students also come here to sit their exams because it has now become too dangerous to go to the university.

I'm working too, in a 'war school' in the new city. It consists of one room in a basement, where we have three classes, three teachers, three blackboards propped up on chairs, all working at the same time. The only light comes from one small window, but we manage splendidly. During this war even the children have matured, become old! The only thing that gives us the strength to go on working is the desire to be of use, to help these poor children to survive. My monthly salary is 3 German marks. A few days ago twenty shells fell all round the school building, but we carried on working as if the noise were nothing to do with us. As if the bombs could not harm us, even though, inside, we are conscious of the terrible tribute they exact from us day after day.

We are accustomed to horror, we are also accustomed to the thought of dying. We have become indifferent, and this strange masochism is the most terrible thing. We have become used to not knowing the meaning of happiness, fortune, life.

Every so often I think how wonderful it would be to escape from this hell, to discover the whereabouts of the escape tunnel. Unfortunately that is impossible, or perhaps I should rather say, it would be impossible for the three of us, your father, sister and myself, all together.

Besides which, to leave Sarajevo now would almost certainly mean we could never return. We would lose everything, the whole of our past lives. Above all, and you know what this would mean for us, it would mean losing our books. And lastly, and perhaps most importantly of all, how could we abandon our friends and relatives and all the others who would be left here to die?

I once went to watch a convoy leaving. I shall never forget the faces of those who were going away, because their expressions revealed not only a haste to be gone from Sarajevo, but an even more desperate haste to get away from the living, guilt-inducing sight of those they were leaving behind in the city.

Here we are all suffering in the same way, irrespective of race, sex, etc. Everyone has a different and terrible story to tell, and there is truth in all of them.

Sarajevo looks very sad. Nearly all the buildings – schools, colleges, blocks of flats, barracks – have been destroyed. Rubble and shell-holes are everywhere. Many people, many of our neighbours, have been killed, some in the fighting, some by snipers, some we know not where.

I am happy to know that you, at least, are not here, even though I miss you dreadfully.

Don't worry too much about us. The fate of each one of us is preordained. Maybe we shall survive the horrors and be together again very soon.

Take great care of my adored grandson.

We send you all our love,

Mamma, and Granny Mira

Sarajevo, 24 August 1993

Good morning, sweetheart,

I hope you managed to understand a few words at least when we spoke on the phone. The line was very bad. The most important thing was that Ingemar is coming to Split and you will be able to contact him. I have asked him to bring me back a box of candles. I expect you think it strange that I should spend so much time talking about water when I speak to you, but for us here it means an unimaginable change in living conditions.

My right arm is getting back to normal. Dragging the cart laden with bins of water had stretched it down to below my knees. I jest, but you can't imagine the relief of being able to 'nurse' my little plants that are now revelling in an irrational quantity of water.

25 August 1993

And once again good morning my love,

In the city, apart from the very occasional car or bicycle, the main form of transport is carts of various kinds. It is incredible how people have managed to transform the most unlikely objects into vehicles for carrying bins of water: from modified pushchairs to incredible constructions fitted with roller skates, or containers with every kind of wheel under the sun.

The other day I saw one made out of an upside-down table with a handle that had once been a vacuum-cleaner hose. I often see skate-boards that boys were playing with not so long ago, now providing a base for weird constructions to which water-bins can be lashed.

Another telling image of our city is provided by the dogs. Even last year many people had abandoned their dogs, either because the owners were dead or because they could no longer feed them. There have always been stray dogs in Sarajevo, but the old strays have mated with dogs of every breed, producing puppies who have also mated, so the city has now been invaded by packs of racially redesigned dogs. Imagine the head of an Alsatian on the legs of a Bulldog, the trunk of a Doberman with the face of a Pekinese. These mixtures sometimes produce beautiful results, in others they might have stepped out of a horror film.

A few days ago or, to be precise, three days ago, I wrote a letter to Henry Kissinger. Don't be surprised at my doing this. I asked him to give constitutional status to the Jews who also live here, because in the final analysis we are the fourth established racial group, and could perhaps put into the balance/contribute/throw onto the scales a little of the good sense that seems to be lacking in the present negotiations. The idea was not my own, but the letter I wrote was.

After all the peace negotiations that drag on and on, I have the impression that this is a war that cannot be won. All we can hope for is to rescue whatever we can.

26 August 1993

Here I am again my darling,

Yesterday I met some people from Mostar. Their stories are monstrous. The city is dying utterly beneath the ruins. I asked them what the situation was like in our own Pocitelj. The Muslims have all gone. All of them, absolutely all, were *driven to Blagaj*. Pocitelj as we knew it no longer exists; it is completely populated by Croats.

What are you doing at this time of day? It's Saturday, and I'm trying to conjure up a mental picture of you. The time is a quarter to nine and I expect you have already finished breakfast. I'm trying hard to imagine Vela Luka as I knew it in the seventies, no, I'm mistaken, the sixties, but I can't. I vaguely remember the promenade, but that's all. It must have changed a lot, too, and I can't pinpoint where your hotel might be.

27 August 1993

I hear that where you are the temperature is 18° and the skies are clear. At least I know what the weather's like around you, but I don't know how you, my only love, are feeling.

Ingemar is leaving not on Saturday but tomorrow, and I haven't finished this letter yet. I'm racking my brain for the most important thing to tell you. I love you, of course.

But I shall not be able to finish this letter that is already so waffling. I shall get up early tomorrow to add a few words. I embrace you my only, much-missed love.

This evening I shall go out on the balcony and look for the stars of the Great Bear, the skies permitting, and when I see the first one I shall think of you, and it won't be the first time I do this. Then I shall slip between the tattered sheets of my bed and I shall be disgustingly alone. And so . . .

28 August 1993

. . . a new dawn will arise. And the sky has granted my wish, the clouds have gone, it is clear and has let me see the stars. Including the one where I often dream that our eyes meet.

My love, I must end this letter that has been, one might say, written at breakneck speed because Svenski is leaving in a few minutes. I kiss you, I kiss you, I kiss you, I miss you so much, look after yourself, my love,

Pavle

Sarajevo, 1 September 1993

Hallo there, my love,

Have I ever told you that I miss you? No? Get away with you! But I miss you terribly, my darling. Lately I kept hoping to find a way for us to be together again, but events have made me lose all hope.

The peace efforts in Geneva continue. My ears are getting to be as big as Dumbo's. I listen to the news in Cyrillic at 7 pm, Bosnian at 8 pm, and Roman at 7 in the morning,* and then try to piece together a composite picture of what's been happening over the past twenty four hours.

---

*The point of Pavle's irony is that although Bosnian (previously called Serbo-Croat) is used in all broadcasts, each faction, in its own bulletins, will put a very different slant on the day's news.

3 September 1993

A new day, a new ribbon for the typewriter (which I can still get, luckily).

I kiss you my darling! And I send you my greetings! I nearly took all the skin off my hands this morning washing a pile of socks. It occurs to me that if there was any justice in the world we should have water and power at the same time once a week, then I could use the washing machine and get rid of all the dirty clothes. Did I tell you that I manage to iron my shirts? When I wash them I dry them on hangers pulling the creases out as much as possible. Then I light the stove and put the coal-iron and the heavy steam-iron on the top. When one is hot I iron away as fast as I possibly can, and when it has cooled I use the other. It's very exciting.

Yesterday I kept thinking that something was missing and couldn't imagine what it was until I remembered I hadn't written to you. The autumnal wildness is upon me, a restlessness and energy that I don't know what to do with. If you were here and times were different we could have gone walking in the mountains. It has been raining and I am wondering what is hiding in the woods of our proud country apart from bandits and mines.

Half past nine and no one's in the office yet. Only you and me. Come on, let's have a cigarette and a cup of coffee, shall we? If you were nearer I'd take you to the theatre this evening. There's a new production of Krlza's 'In Agony'.

My daydreams have brought bad luck. Just at this moment the bombardment has started up again so I shall have to break off.

My love, my love, my love, I miss you so much. Write to me,

Pavle

Sarajevo, 27 September 1993

Beloved,

I am devising a nice, if strange, letter because it looks as if Ingemar, who got back yesterday evening, will have to leave again tomorrow morning. This took me by surprise but there is nothing I can do about it.

What are you doing, my darling? Here the days pass slowly and, as usual, senselessly. It is all too much. We had to put the clocks back this morning by one hour, but an hour, methinks, is not enough. One ought to be able to turn them back to April two years ago and maybe further still. I find it all very depressing, and if I begin to think about happy days in the past that is now so distant, the uncertainty of the future becomes even more unbearable.

When I enter the flat and look around me, everything is sad and empty. My den, without you, my she-wolf, is only a hole to hide in, not a home. Every now and then I stop and look at the things around me, I think, I dream, and feel alone to the point of madness. Everything is there and waiting for you. Yes, this is only a sleeping-den, nothing else. And I may have to abandon it for ever at any moment.

What are the clouds and the sea doing? And do seagulls still follow the ships? And do you love me?

And why are you not here with me? I'll finish this letter tomorrow morning and then hand it over. I hug you!

28 September 1993

Good morning, my only love,

I don't know what's going on in the city. They're shooting, shooting, shooting. They've killed two local government officials. In brief, there is never any peace.

I must finish because Ingemar's about to go. He'll put my letter in with his papers and post it in Split.

Don't worry. A big, big hug. Look after yourself.

Pavle

And there are no empty worlds:
That of which we are not aware
Is not non-being
But being without ourselves.

Even the most far-distant future
Has a future
That can hear
The voice of its own future.

                              Nikola Nescovic
                         Sarajevo, November 1992

Nikola Nescovic was one of Sarajevo's most prominent architects, responsible for many public buildings erected in the seventies and eighties including several schools and Sarajevo's airport, Butmir. Three of the letters he wrote to his two daughters, refugees in Milan, are printed in this collection (dated 14 October, 11 and 19 February). The last of these arrived at the beginning of March, shortly after the daughters had received news of his death in Sarajevo on February 20th. Nescovic, sixty-six at the time of his death, was diabetic. The non-availability of insulin during the siege was responsible for the lesion to his finger mentioned in the letter of 11 February. The finger was later amputated.

People of Sarajevo

A Postscript

When I was working on the Italian edition of this book in February 1993, the faces of all those who had written the letters were unknown to me. At that stage I had only met the recipients, refugees in Italy and France, with whom I had managed to establish contact. I was unaware that on every subsequent journey to Sarajevo I would be carrying letters, parcels and medicines back to the besieged city, and that many of the people whose handwriting and signatures appeared on those torn, crumpled pieces of paper would acquire faces, voices, homes, scents, and stories to tell. Sometimes they would be miraculously unharmed, but often were no more. Every time I left Sarajevo I left behind ghostly forms more emaciated than before, and every time I was swallowed up by the noisy maw of the shuddering Hercules and found myself at last flying towards the safety of the clouds, high above the deadly Butmir runway, I told myself: 'I am never going to return. It's too dangerous. I have three children who need me.' And every time, once back in the lap of 'peace' those eyes and those faces haunted me with increasing force and it simply became morally unacceptable to know that they were there, enduring the horrific circumstances shown for a few seconds each day on my television in Italy, only 50 minutes flying time away. So I would ask UNICEF to send me out again, and would return to Sarajevo . . . with letters, parcels and medicines. I was not always able to deliver them into the hands for which they were intended. In March 1993, when the air-lift was suspended, I attempted the land route, but because of bomb-shattered roads, fighting and a snow-storm that stopped us between Gornj Vakuf and Vitez, the journey took six days (although it is only 250 km between Split and Sarajevo) and we were subjected to several road-blocks as a consequence. I was carrying two hundred letters. All were confiscated. I was unable to deliver a single one.

I learnt to hide them better before my next trip and, with the help of UNICEF's wonderful personnel, to consign them into the hands of those who awaited them with such longing. Without UNICEF's help I should have been completely defeated, as tracing the recipients in a city that is twelve km long and three wide, with no telephones, no vehicles on the roads apart from tanks and armoured cars (in the service of the UN, the press, humanitarian organizations or agencies), where not a drop of petrol is to be had, where there are no public utilities, no shops, bars or restaurants, where walking down a street involves a game of Russian roulette with snipers and flying fragments of bombs, shells or whatever, and where there have been no postal services for more than two years, is, as one might imagine, no easy task. And not made any easier for someone like myself who does not speak the local language, called 'Serbo-Croat' when I was first in Sarajevo, in 1992, but now proudly referred to only as 'Bosnian'.

No, I had as yet met none of the writers of the letters when the Italian edition was preparing, but I had met other people in Sarajevo. I had spent hours in their shelters, had drunk their coffee, listened to their stories, admired their dignity, their courage, the great courtesy and the humanity that they managed to retain intact despite the daily horrors that surrounded them.

Jenina

The corner room on the second floor of the hospital in Kosevo was bathed in sunshine that poured through two high windows, the only windows in the building to have remained intact.

'Now we shall pay a visit to Jenina,' the journalist had said as we climbed the stairs. 'She is a model of strength of character. She's been here for months and her smile has kept everyone else's spirits up.'

Jenina was sitting on the edge of an iron bedstead pushed against the wall. In front of her, a nurse held two plastic bowls of water in which Jenina was bathing the stumps of legs that had been severed half way up her thigh.

Jenina was nineteen, blue-eyed, with blond hair tied in a pony tail high on her head and a brace on her teeth that sparkled as she smiled her delight at our visit.

'Is there anything you want, Jenina? Anthing we can we get for you?'

'Oh yes,' she replied jokingly, 'An orange, lots of oranges!'

It is not easy to get to Kosevo every day, and three days later, when we returned with the oranges, we were told that Jenina had been discharged from hospital. One of the nurses had her home address. It took a while to find her in the Moslem quarter of Bascarsija with its steep, narrow streets and its nativity-scene houses, but then we met up with some others on their way to welcome Jenina back home.

Three months earlier, Jenina and her sister had gone, as they did every day, to fetch bread. They were standing in the queue when the shelling started. Three members of her family were killed outright. Her sister was unhurt. Jenina was hit in the legs.

Leaving our boots and shoes outside the door, we went into the small kitchen. She was sitting on an L-shaped sofa. Neighbours had brought a few flowers.

Flowers were the first thing I saw as my plane was landing in Sarajevo. Roses, a bed of roses among the shattered remains of the airport. Roses of delicate hue swaying to the roar of Hercules engines, the crackle of gunfire and the frenzied shouts of command. Someone had planted them and someone was apparently watering them.

Jenina was wearing a light blue sweater and smiling; her mother, father and sister were smiling; the neighbours were smiling.

We were given Turkish coffee in the customary little cups, and a precious tin of dunje, quinces in syrup, was opened. Jenina's mother signalled to me with a nod. I followed her out of the room but as I didn't know her language we couldn't speak. She looked at me, wept and dried her eyes on her apron.

Jenina spoke good English: 'Come here, close to me,' she said. 'I want to ask you a question, but you must tell me the truth. You said you have a daughter the same age as me. Now tell me, if this happened to your daughter, what would you feel inside?'

'Anger,' I said, 'a rage so tremendous it would choke me.'

'You know,' she went on, 'at the hospital they said I was good because I smiled, so I felt it was my duty to go on smiling. Here at home everyone pretends to be jolly. They avoid mentioning my legs. But I can't go on like this. I want to howl and cry. Sometimes I think I am going mad.'

Then I told her about Oliver Sacks, the English neurologist I had interviewed a year earlier in New York. Sacks explains that the loss of a limb causes severe neurological, as well as physical, trauma because the ideal image of our body that we have always thought of and continue to think of as intact, has been put at risk.

'Go on talking,' said Jenina. 'Tell me more.'

And later, when I was saying goodbye, she said, 'Please come again, come and talk to me before I leave. They've put me on the military aircraft waiting list. They say they are going to send me to Sweden to be fitted with artificial legs . . .'

As I was going out of the door she called me back. 'You know, I want to continue with my studies, get a degree, have a boyfriend, marry and have children.'

I was unable to return to Jenina. In Sarajevo you cannot move around freely.

Back in Italy I was able to get news of her just once. It was January, and Jenina was still in Sarajevo.

Dzirlo Sakir

We were in Titova Street when Sakir called out to us. We crossed the road to him.

'The old doctor died yesterday.'

'What? We saw him only three days ago. He had so many plans . . .'

'A sniper . . . He was walking to the hospital.'

In the graveyard on the hill, among the ancient Moslem misrham, there was a new grave, a mound of earth surmounted by a small wooden rectangle bearing his name.

'Please, as you have a film in your camera, would you take a photograph?' Sakir asked. 'Then his son would have something to remember him by. He lives in Texas, and we will try to let him know.'

The old doctor's home had gone, as had his operating theatre at the hospital. I took a photograph of the grave, then Sakir invited us to his apartment.

Before the war Sakir worked for the Sarajevo electricity authority. Now he dashes about all day trying to repair cables damaged
by the bombs. He has four children and a beautiful wife, Amra,
who is an architect. The flat has a large sitting room with a bay
window overlooking Titova Street, right in the city centre, next to
the market. The eldest daughter, Meliha, seventeen, curvaceous,
with a mass of wavy hair, is considered the most promising young
pianist of the former Yugoslavia. Sakir's two sons are playing the
guitar as we enter. As soon as she sees us, Amra starts preparing
coffee on a little ring in a corner of the room. Sakir speaks, the
members of his family listen deferentially. He does not want his
family to die in Sarajevo. He is doing all he can to get them out.
But how? And where would they go?

And what about their home, this lovely flat furnished with
Turkish antiques lovingly collected by Amra over the years?
They will have to leave all this behind them. But the walls are
now comprehensively punctured by shrapnel, and last night two
whole floors of the house opposite were completely destroyed.

'Meliha, would you play the piano for us?'

A vase of yellow flowers stands on the grand piano.

The Moslems of Bosnia have no alternative homeland.

Meliha plays, gunfire crackles in the street outside, darkness is
falling and the flame of the candle on the piano wavers. Meliha
stops in the middle of a piece.

'I can't continue. The piano is out of tune and I haven't heard
from the tuner for two months . . .'

'It doesn't matter, you're terribly good. Do you manage to
practise every day? How do you arrange your time?'

'We don't make any plans when we wake up in the morning.
Nobody knows what will happen from one minute to the next or
even if we shall still be alive by the evening.'

Her little sister Leyla, who does not speak English, watches us
and smiles.

Ademir Kenovic and Abdulah Sidran

Ademir and Sidran had the room next to mine. They had a
hairdryer, and on the few occasions I managed to procure water

to wash my hair, I went to their room to dry it. There was only one power-point still working, and to use the dryer we had to disconnect the lamp. So we chatted by candlelight. Ademir is a film director and Sidran a great poet. He is known to the world as the writer of screenplays for Emir Kustorica's films (*When father was away on business* and *Do you remember Dolly Bell*, etc.) but would rather not talk about it. Kustorica is in Hollywood, too far away from what is happening in Sarajevo. In fact Sidran only speaks Bosnian, so we can only communicate through Ademir, who speaks both English and French. Sidran must be a wit, because when he is among his admirers in the dining room downstairs, his remarks are constantly greeted by laughter. The first time I saw him – a small man dressed in black, wearing an oriental jacket, with long white hair and a little pointed beard, also white, giving him a satanic air – I took him for a magician or conjuror.

Ademir and Sidran are preparing to shoot a film, a real film as opposed to a documentary, in the streets of Sarajevo.

Ademir has beautiful hands, he is pale and so thin that I am sometimes afraid his legs might snap under him.

His wife lives with their daughter in Prague, out of danger. He has chosen to remain in Sarajevo 'to the end'.

He lent me his diary to read.

'. . . today is the first of July. A man is walking ahead of me down Miskin Street. Under his arm he carries a parcel wrapped in newspaper. The man stops, discards the wrapping, pulls out a pistol and shoots himself in the head . . .'

'. . . it is afternoon, the sun is about to set, in front of me I see the hill where, three days ago, a bomb fell on my mother's house and killed her. In our home, in the very room where, on a June afternoon many years ago, I introduced her so proudly to my professor, Nikola Koljevic, the guru of my adolescence, the man whom I admired more than any other, who taught me to love poetry, who made me understand Shakespeare . . . Three days ago Nikola Koljevic, the architect of Etnicko Cisenje (Ethnic Cleansing) gave the order to fire the bomb that killed my mother . . .'

He also showed me his screenplay for *Film interdit*, translated into French because it is to be produced in France. 'Two old friends, Grand Père Edo and Grand Père Mirko, left on their own in Sarajevo, try to cope with the war situation. Edo, who is seventy two, has lost heart and wants to stay home and die, while Mirko, who is four years older, tries to rouse him, keeps himself busy, goes out looking for firewood, bread, water . . . One day Mirko fails to return and Edo is forced to go and look for him. People tell him his friend is dead. It is dark when he finally finds him, in the mortuary. He sees him . . . and Mirko raises himself, comes towards him and tells him that he will help him organize the funeral, not an easy thing to do in Sarajevo in the winter of 1992. Chatting pleasantly, the two friends, one dead, one alive, start out on a long walk through the streets of Sarajevo . . .'

Ademir wants to start shooting after Christmas. Actor friends from all over Europe have offered their services, but he has had to refuse them. He cannot, he explains, assume the responsibility for their coming to Sarajevo. It's too dangerous.

Saturday, 7 November 1992. There were rumours yesterday that the citizens of Sarajevo had taken the desperate decision to march in a tightly-knit band towards Ilidza and to break out of the city guns or no guns.

It is now clear that the world will do nothing to help Sarajevo, where people continue to die like rats in a trap.

The rendezvous was at dawn, in the open space by the old bakery. Thousands were expected, but when the mist started to clear we saw only a hundred or so. Fear had gained the upper hand, and only a handful of desperate people set out on the march. The sun shone but it was extremely cold.

The journalists and film-makers covering the march sweated at the thought of the massacre that could start from one minute to the next.

Nothing happened.

A few trucks were dragged across the road, a few machine guns were aimed. Crushed men and women, dragging handcarts piled with their household goods, turned back weeping.

The Moslems of Bosnia have no alternative homeland.

The Swimmer

Every morning she jogged around the track circling the grass centre of the stadium now being transformed into a graveyard. She was seventeen, tall, with almond-shaped eyes and hair the colour of dark copper. Silver medal for swimming (I do not remember in which category) at the last Olympics. Since the beginning of the war she had lost two teeth through malnutrition. She asked us if we had any vitamin tablets. She could move faster, she said, than the snipers' bullets. For five months it had been impossible to swim in Sarajevo. Running was essential; without running she would begin to die.

Peter, the German photographer, brought her to the hotel. In the evening she would appear at the journalists' long table and happily eat the insipid fare served up by the Holiday Inn. Peter departed. On the last evening she wore a plum-coloured, almost black lipstick.

We never saw her again, not even on the jogging track.

Flowers had been lovingly placed on every new grave in Sarajevo. Ignoring the gunfire, women knelt to tend the graves, caress the flowers.

The crosses carried, in black, the name and year of birth, invariably followed by '1992'. Except the most recent ones, which only had '92', because the stock of black numbers was running low and it was necessary to save on them where possible.

Even the few tree trunks that remained in the cemeteries were decorated with little bunches of flowers.

Desanka Dakovic and Nada Kaluderovic

Desanka was the daughter. Twenty six years old, six months pregnant, she stood beside her mother who was seated on the two black cases into which the family had crammed everything it could before leaving never to return. The long yellow station building offered no protection, since bombing had destroyed everything except the façade. People were huddled on the steps to the entrance that were covered with broken glass that glinted in the sun. Children were playing with the glass. Chunks of plaster littered the whole of the station approach where, for three days, Serb civilians with permits to leave Sarajevo had been waiting in vain, in freezing temperatures, for the promised coaches that never arrived.

The 'others', Moslems and Croats, had only waited until the afternoon, outside Tito's barracks on the other side of the road, before piling into coaches carrying them away into the unknown. Families had been divided by a stroke of the pen between the road going east, towards Spalato, and that going west, towards Belgrade. Nearly fifty per cent of the families in Sarajevo are mixed: Croats married to Serbs, Moslems to Croats, Serbs to Moslems. A plan to divide Sarajevo according to ethnic groups would have to provide for walls cutting bedrooms into two.

And mixed marriages – two or three every month – have continued to be celebrated even since the outbreak of war. Desanka's husband was a Moslem. She hadn't seen him for four months. The child she was carrying would be their first.

Desanka was wearing a black overcoat and a voluminous light-blue sweater. A psychology graduate, she had specialized in the problems of mentally handicapped children. Nada, her mother, was a writer and former BBC correspondent in Sarajevo. For thirty years she had run a school for autistic children. Mother and daughter had worked as a team.

'In Belgrade,' said Desanka, 'I shall still be involved with child psychiatry. There will be a great need for it. After the war, seventy per cent of the children in Sarajevo will have severe psychological problems.'

The mother's hair was half white and half purplish-red, meeting in a straight line where it had begun to grow and she had been unable to dye it any longer.

She was crying. 'If only I could stop crying and sleep . . .'

Thirty years, she said, thirty years of hard work to construct a glass dome around 'her' children. Exhausting work requiring infinite patience and a delicacy of touch that allowed for no slips. The joy of success when they managed to make the first tiny crack in the shell of isolation surrounding those young sick minds. The first contact, the thrill of having found a way to help . . . And all destroyed by the first grenade on the morning of 6 April 1992.

'For autistic children the slightest disturbance can be enough to send them back into their shell for ever. The shots fired that morning destroyed the whole of my life's work.'

'How many children were there?'

'Twenty-eight.'

'And where are they now?'

'I don't know, I haven't been able to find out anything more about them.'

The glass dome had been shattered. Love had been unable to protect them.

*Since 29 May 1992 there have always been flowers in Miskin Street
in Sarajevo. Fresh flowers laid in a long line on the ground just
where the shells exploded around people queueing for bread. The
city is nothing but a heap of smoke-blackened rubble . . . where do
these gaily-coloured flowers come from, and how can they grow?*

*President Mitterand, Elie Wisel, Dr Boutros-Ghali, Bernard
Kouchner and Bernard Henri-Levy have all paused in front of
those flowers to pay their respects . . . Miskin Street is included
in all the 'tours' arranged for world leaders who come on their
compassionate visits to Sarajevo.*

*These 'tours' follow a standard procedure. After arriving in a
Hercules at Butmir airport in the late morning, the 'personality',
suitably protected by bullet-proof jacket and helmet, is conveyed
to UNPROFOR headquarters in an armoured vehicle for a press
conference. He or she is then driven, again in an armoured car (for
the occupants this is like being in a submarine: you sit in a row,
knees up to your mouth, squinting at a tiny bit of sky through the
port-hole at the top), to the presidential palace.*

*Audiences are invariably held in the drawing room on the first
floor with yellow satin armchairs and sofas.*

The conversation is tense.

Then comes the procession to pay homage in Miskin Street.

CNN and EBU immortalize the visitors.

*Finally it's back to the armoured cars and full speed to Butmir,
because take-offs are only possible in daylight.*

*The day before an official visit there is always great activity to
clear the streets of rubble, but the flowers in Miskin Street are not
put there for the occasion. Fresh ones appear every day.*

The Young Couple

I saw the dog before I saw them. A black Dobermann tied to a pillar
at the entrance to the police station in Ilidza. I went up and stroked
it. Dobermanns hold no fear for me, my daughter has one. This
was a bitch, with restless black eyes and teats swollen with milk.

The young couple came down the steps escorted by three soldiers
carrying Skorpions.

They saw me stroking the dog. 'She's not ours,' they explained.
'She belongs to a friend who asked us to bring her with us. She's
the Yugoslav champion bitch.'

The woman was a Croat of twenty-four; she had a brown jacket and big green eyes. He was twenty-seven and a Serb.

They had arrived on foot from Sarajevo, the first to have succeeded in eight months.

'Didn't you come under fire? . . . What time was it? When?'

'We walked.'

'But where? Where did you cross the lines?'

They looked exhausted, as if the effort to speak was almost too much for them.

'We can't tell you. It could cost the lives of many people.'

'Will others try?'

'We can't even tell you that.'*

'Where will you go now?'

'It's not over yet. For the moment we have to wait for the authorities in Ilidza to make their decisions.'

We were on our way to Kiseljak and would like to have given them a lift. As it was we had to leave them there, suspended between freedom and imprisonment, after risking so much.

We drove up into the mountains. Suddenly the noise of shooting and the piles of rubble were left behind, replaced by green fields, streams, trees dressed in the red-gold of autumn, placid cows, picturesque chalets and silence.

It was dumbfounding! Less than twenty kilometres away there was hunger, death, never-ending terror. But Kiseljak, had it not been for the noisy coming and going of tanks with their fluttering blue UN flags, might have been in Switzerland.

You can sit in the sun on the terrace of a restaurant, order a meal, enter a shop, even buy ORANGES!

We filled our cans with petrol and, taking advantage of a UN convoy en route to Sarajevo, set out on the return journey.

The young couple stepped out of the sentry-post at the top of the mountain. The sun was setting. They recognized us. She was

---

*The secret route mentioned here is no longer secret. In August 1993 the New York Times even published an article about it, revealing that the citizens of Sarajevo, working for month after month – WITH THEIR BARE HANDS – had dug a tunnel 700 metres long beneath the airport runway. So low and narrow that only one person can use it at a time, this tunnel was used to convey supplies of food and materials for heating to the outlying districts of Dobrinja and Butmir throughout the winter.

weeping for joy, while he, holding the dog's leash, was very pale. The formalities were over, they had been allowed through, they were free!

'We shall go to Canada,' he said.

'Have you got any family or friends there?'

'No, but I shall find a job.'

'What did you do in Sarajevo?'

'For the last six months my job has been working out a way to escape. I don't want to remember any further back than that.'

They were both graduates.

'Stretno! Good luck!'

'Stretno to you too!' they replied.

We drove back into Sarajevo, ghostly in the moonlight. Not a car on the streets, not a lighted window, not a single street lamp.

'It reminds me of Peking during the T'ien-an-Men Square business,' someone said.

The Two Old Ladies

They had carried – I don't know how – a chair to the open space in front of the station. This chair had very long legs carved in Tyrolean-Baroque style. The two ladies never left each other for a second, they were always together and seemed to know no one else among the refugees who had already been waiting to leave for several days. White-haired and very upright, they walked backwards and forwards on the first morning, chatting to each other. Later, they took it in turns to sit on the tall chair. On the ground beside them was their luggage: a dark green suitcase and a holdall with United Colours Of Benetton on it in strident letters.

One of the ladies was wearing a grey suit and a Loden overcoat, the other wore a black fur coat. I saw them cover their faces whenever they noticed a television lens pointing in their direction.

By the third day many of the refugees had left, but the old ladies were still there with their chair and their Benetton holdall. Their eyes were red and they were making much use of handkerchiefs. They were no longer talking, even to each other.

On Wednesday I saw they had gone and I was glad. Someone said they had left with the convoy for Belgrade.

On Thursday the 'France Presse' photographer who had covered the convoy was back in the hotel. I asked him how things had gone.

'The Serbs held up the coaches all night saying they had to check the documents, but eventually they let them through.'

'All of them? They didn't detain any?'

'They were all allowed through. Ah, do you remember those two old ladies?'

'Yes.'

When the coach arrived in Pale everyone got out except them. Someone got back in to see what had happened. They were dead.'

When the television centre was opened in 1984 in time for the Winter Olympics, the citizens of Sarajevo dubbed it 'the bunker'. And in fact the long parallelepiped, three storeys of dark grey concrete almost devoid of windows, had little charm. Now, in the autumn of 1992, one wonders if the architect was clairvoyant. Knocked about, battered and dented it may be, but the building still stands amid the wreckage of Dzemala Bijedica Avenue, known as 'snipers' avenue', and its walls of concrete sixty centimetres thick hide and protect a veritable 'bunker' from which, day and night, a handful of men transmit to the world those pictures of Sarajevo that darken and disturb our evening news programmes.

Television crews on assignments in Sarajevo arrive with a great squeal of brakes from the road at the rear, leap from their vehicles and run at full tilt through the entrance controlled by armed guards into the long, dark corridor on the left. Leaving behind the now unusable film studios that stand dark and silent, they arrive at the heart of the EBU, the European Broadcasting Union, a pool of international television companies formed in the summer of 1992. The BBC, CNN, Visnews and Antenne 2 were its first members; the others joined later. In four small, dark rooms the crews eat, sleep, broadcast and edit news of the latest tragedy as it is brought in, in an unending stream, by exhausted cameramen. On the makeshift plywood walls of the corridor, someone has painted a blue sky and some enormous crimson roses.

'Stop, cut, go back, forward, a bit more . . . that's enough.'

In front of the small screens editors put together sequences showing the reality of life in Sarajevo, compressed into the few,

*exceedingly expensive seconds of air time between the black letters
– and black humour – of the logo: EBU Boum! * SARAJEVO *
Boum!*

*These are all young people who resist the demoralizing effect of
what is happening 'outside' by clinging to their sense of humour.
They have even designed a T-shirt overprinted with the words: 'I
survived Sarajevo 1992 . . .' followed by: '. . . once . . .', blank
space, 'twice . . .', blank space. No one would even contemplate
adding: 'three times . . .'.*

*I bought one of these myself, thinking that, rather than tempt
fate, I would wear it only when I got home. When I pulled it out
of my knapsack in Milan, it stank of fuel oil and paint, and when
I washed it all the colours ran. So I was never able to put a tick
in the first blank space to advertise the fact that I had survived
'once'.*

Eli and Doron

They were not native to Sarajevo. They came from Jerusalem. They
had come to help and they did everything together. They spoke
a lot about the work of their organization (the American Joint
Distribution Committee) and little about themselves. 'We have no
name,' they said. 'We are a team.' We later learnt that this 'team'
of two had organized the evacuation from Ethiopia, in 1992, of
14,000 Jews in twenty-four hours! Operation SOLOMON it was
called.

In Sarajevo they were preparing another rescue mission, not
only for Jews this time.

'Whoever knocks on this door,' says Ivan Ceresnjes, a forty-
seven-year-old architect and head of the synagogue (there has been
no rabbi in Sarajevo since 1968), 'we only ask them two questions:
"What do you need?" and "How many are you?" Nothing else.'

That door was 25 metres from the river Miljacka and 250 from
the firing line. Inside, they served hot soup every day at noon, and
then distributed food and medicines.

Eli and Doron came and went in the winding passageways of the
old pink-washed synagogue, especially by night. In a little room on
the first floor they took turns to operate the radio powered by a
generator running on fuel oil.

By dawn on D-day there was already a crowd in front of the synagogue.

Sarajevo was the only city in Europe where Jews had lived for centuries without there being a ghetto. The word 'anti-semitism' was unknown. As was 'racism'.

'Today we're sending out the old, the sick and the crippled. About six hundred of them, people who couldn't survive the winter. We'll try and help those who remain by getting in supplies of food and medicines.'

'But where are you sending these six hundred people?'

'We are already in contact with five hundred families in Austria, Germany, the United States and Canada. They will take them in. As Jews we feel a duty to help others, because so many people helped us after the war. And besides, we want to prove to the world that the horrors of the Holocaust will never be repeated.'

Cripples in wheelchairs, coughing men and women wrapped in shawls wait, with shining eyes, in the rain. They dare not hope. Eli and Doron roam around nervously, casting unfriendly glances at television cameramen. It's ten o'clock and there is no sign of the convoy.

A man with a greenish complexion wipes the sweat off his forehead repeatedly.

'Are you leaving, or are you here to see someone off?'

His name is Ognjen Turtkovic, he's a musician.

'I have tuberculosis. I am going to Ljubljana for treatment, but I want to come back to Sarajevo as soon as possible, because this is my city.'

High up on a little balcony, sitting on a chair squeezed between piles of firewood and plastic dustbins filled with water, a man is playing a violin. The notes are faint, barely audible.

'I'm very sad to be leaving Sarajevo,' continues Ognjen, 'because I have to leave my music behind. I am trying to rescue the heritage of popular music, which is extremely rich here. I've worked in all the different media. I had Umberto Eco's *Opera aperta* published in Sarajevo. I know everything he has written. He's a media genius.'

A column of eight coaches and three trucks materializes as if by magic. The people gather round and watch with uplifted faces as pasta, sugar, oil, coffee and flour are unloaded . . . and they smile.

'On my way here this morning I was afraid,' says a journalist working for Israeli television who has been held up for a week in Kiseljak, 'because I realized that what has happened in Sarajevo could break out at any moment, anywhere: WAR BETWEEN THE SECOND AND SIXTEENTH ARRONDISSEMENTS! In Paris!'

The park beside the barracks was carpeted with wet yellow leaves. People were hurrying down the side paths carrying plastic containers and buckets and then queueing patiently to await their turn to fill them at the drinking fountain. They were crossing the river not by the big road bridge but by a footbridge a hundred metres further downstream. The footbridge was awkward and could only be used by one person at a time, clinging to a rope handrail; but perhaps it was less exposed to sniper fire. The big bridge, imposing but deserted, is generally referred to as 'The bridge of Gavrilo Princip'.

Princip was not his real surname, only a nickname, but his real name was never known and it is as Princip that he passed into history. A poor man, or rather a boy, of nineteen, he had come down from the mountains at dawn on 28 June 1914 wearing a short black jacket decorated with little bells and carrying a pistol in his pocket. He probably had no idea of what to do with the pistol.

The story is a strange one of fate and coincidence. Everybody had warned the Grand Duke Franz Ferdinand d'Este (the unpopular sole heir of the Hapsburg empire) against going to Sarajevo. But he was stubborn, and the ageing emperor Franz Josef, to whom his nephew's actions were of minor interest, had not opposed him.

There had been signs of unrest since the morning of that fateful June day, and a shot had been heard among the crowd, though the gunman was never identified. At breakfast in the Town Hall the military governor, General Potiorek, advised the Archduke to cut his visit short. The Archduke refused, and, as a precaution, it was decided that the official route should be changed. In the ensuing haste, however, no one thought of informing the driver who, having crossed the second bridge, turned round to follow the escorting car.

'What are you doing?' roared Potiorek, bringing his hand down heavily on the man's shoulder. The driver, confused, braked to

a halt. So the open car carrying the Archduke Ferdinand and his wife Sophie stood in the road, quite still and dead opposite the spot where the luckless Gavrilo Princip was standing on the pavement. Princip fired. 'Sophie, Sophie, live for our children's sake!' murmured Franz Ferdinand before collapsing. 'I love you,' she replied, throwing herself over him, and died with the second bullet.

On the spot where Gavrilo Princip was standing as he fired the shot, the imprints of his feet, carved in marble, can still be seen. Or rather, they could be seen, because a shell left a crater in the pavement, scattering fragments of the footprints over a wide area. I picked one up. The marble is olive green.

'Look,' said a shocked Rebecca West to her husband during her 1937 visit to the Balkans,* 'the river at Sarajevo runs red, as red as blood.'

Meliha and Leyla

Meliha was standing at the window.

'Come on up!' she called. It was ten o'clock in the morning, and she and Leyla were alone in the house. The apartment was dark and freezing.

'Don't take off your shoes,' she said, 'it's too cold.'

But I removed them all the same. To step into a Moslem home with shoes on one's feet would be like saying: the war has succeeded in destroying everything; hope is dead.

Leyla jumped up and down and smiled. Her cheeks were as round as apples: evidently the Dzirlo family were doing everything to ensure that the little girl, at least, did not go short of food.

'Come in here,' they said, picking their way between buckets of water lined up on the floor towards a small room at the back where a stove was sputtering. In the middle of the room were three mattresses covered in antique carpets. Leyla curled up on one and a black and white kitten jumped onto her lap. She buried her face in its fur. The schools had been closed since May and she had not been out of the house for months.

'We've been expecting you for ages because of the cake!'

*See *Black Lamb and Grey Falcon*, published 1942.

'What cake?' I asked.

'Oh no, didn't they tell you? Mamma expected you on Wednesday. She actually managed to make a cake. We looked at it for three days and then we ate it. We finished the last bit yesterday. It was delicious.'

A cake in Sarajevo ... with no eggs, no butter ... no oven to bake it in ... they must have mobilized the entire district ...

'What do they say in your country about what is happening in Sarajevo?' asked Meliha, pouring me a cup of Turkish coffee. And then, without waiting for a reply: 'You know, our father is so disappointed with Mr Bush. He expected the Americans to help us. He even tried to speak to him!'

From what I could gather, one night in May the Dzirlo family was woken with a jump, not by the noise of the bombing, which they were used to, but by the sound of Sakir's vehement voice. 'Hello! Is that the White House?' he was shouting into the phone. 'Put me on to the President! I must speak to him. We're being slaughtered here. We're all being slaughtered! Can't you hear the shooting? He must hear it too ...'

Having failed with the phone, he began to write letters. 'They said he was a good man,' he told his children. But since October he had not even mentioned the name of President Bush.

I told Meliha about the Jews. 'They're fantastic,' she remarked. 'Everyone else talks and talks but nothing happens. The Jews keep quiet and no one knows what they've done until it's all over. There was a boy, a Moslem friend of mine, who used to bring us a copy of 'Oslobodjenje' every day. Then one day he didn't turn up, nor the next. I began to worry about him, but then I heard he had been spirited out of Sarajevo, by the Jews. I had seen him the day before, we had chatted for hours, but he had said nothing about it.'

Leyla got up and put the kitten out of the window, on the roof.

I was going. As I stood in the doorway she seized my arm. 'When are you coming back? When are you coming to see us again?' She smiled and dimples appeared on her cheeks.

I had drunk seven cups of coffee. I stepped out into the square surrounding the covered market where people were gazing at the stalls in a kind of trance. There was nothing, or hardly anything, there. Two old shoes, three pairs of laces, a Bic lighter, a pair of hand-knitted socks, a corkscrew. The only edible commodity was a few bunches of vivid green nettles. A blonde woman clutching a German banknote was bargaining for one of the bunches. I pulled out my camera, but then put it back in my pocket.

A queue that tailed back over three blocks was waiting in front of Caritas.

I hadn't told Meliha that it was my birthday. She would have been even more upset that they hadn't saved a single slice of cake for me!

The Young Chetnik

Ademir took me to the prison where a Chetnik boy of twenty-two who had been arrested two days earlier was being questioned. Convinced that Sarajevo was in Serb hands, he had been driving through the city in a jeep with two other soldiers on board.

Shaven-headed, with his strangely oriental eyes gazing into the void, he calmly described cutting the throats of twenty-nine Moslems. Kneeling on the floor, he even demonstrated how he had immobilized his victims with one hand while cutting their throats, with a single clean stroke, with the other. They had made him practise on pigs, he told us, but it was a bit difficult for him, being left-handed. 'But how do you know that your victims were all Moslems?'

'Because I asked them their names.' And he repeated the twenty-nine names, slowly, like telling the beads of a rosary. 'Ahmed, Osman, Kasim, Amir ... I remember them because I dream about them every night. I also dream about the noise.'

'What noise?'

'The noise of spurting blood. It sickens me.'

'Why do you hate Moslems?'

'I don't hate them. They were my best friends before the war. I've got a sister in Sarajevo who is married to a Moslem.'

'Then why ... ?'

'Because I was told to do it.'

'And if they told you to kill your sister's husband?'

'If it was an order I would have to obey it.'*

At night, if the shooting stopped you woke up with the feeling that something was wrong. Silence in Sarajevo grated on the ear like a wrong note. You waited in the dark, ears pricked, listening. Then boom, boom, it started up again and you went back to sleep soothed as if by a lullaby.

But if you went to the hospital the next day, you saw the deadly effect of such a cradle song. Anxious stretcher-bearers about their work; relatives holding the hands of wounded people staring wide-eyed out of chalk-white faces; silent men and women with glistening eyes packing the benches outside the operating theatres; mothers with their children muffled in blood-soaked sheets; exhausted doctors, nurses with red-splashed uniforms, orderlies carrying bins overflowing with gauzes and bandages saturated with blood that was still bright red.

Looking for a patient, I took a wrong turning and found myself in the vast kitchens. Empty. Not a crust of bread remained.

Avdo Kapidzic

Of all the eyes that were gazing imploringly at me having seen the label 'Unprofor, Press Accreditation' on my chest, I cannot tell why I turned to his. Ardo had a sweet smile and gentle eyes. He was eighteen, with dark-blond hair and an exceptionally beautiful face. His right arm, attached to the drip, was resting on a pillow, and a urine bag was taped to the side of the bed with a piece of sticking plaster. He smiled at me.

Using gestures, I asked about his injuries.

He lifted the sheet with his left hand. His legs, from the groin down, were missing.

Pointing to himself and shrugging his shoulders, he said, 'Soldier'. Then he lowered the sheet and smiled again.

I stayed there, standing beside him, holding his hand.

*At his trial in Sarajevo, which lasted two weeks, this boy, Borislav Herak, confessed to the murder of thirty-two Moslems (including one whole family of ten) and to the rape and murder of twelve women besides. He stated that he had been acting under orders. I was present in the courtroom when he was sentenced to death on 30 March 1993. A. C.

Before leaving I gave him my card: it was all I had. He looked at it carefully before placing it on the locker. 'Vrati se. Come back, please come back . . .'

Everyone in Sarajevo says 'Come back'. Come back to visit us in our cellars, our shelters, our silent days of waiting, imprisoned, compelled to serve a sentence for which we do not know the reason. Don't forget us. DON'T LEAVE US ALL ALONE. DON'T ABANDON US.

The day before my departure I went to see Avdo in hospital. It was the only promise I was able to keep in Sarajevo.

This time he had two friends beside his bed. They had brought him some comics. The girl, possibly his girlfriend, was very pretty and spoke English: 'Avdo told us about you'.

I had brought a bar of chocolate and three oranges, given me by a journalist.

The girl interpreted for me.

'Avdo, do you feel like telling me how it happened?'

'It was the 25th October at 11 o'clock in the morning. The soldier next to me was hit in the head. We were on a hill. I felt nothing at all, no pain. It was like flying through the air. It was almost pleasant. Then the pain began. Very bad, not in my legs, but in my stomach.'

'Who found you?'

'My father, who was a soldier too. He and the other soldiers carried me to hospital. While they were operating I was clinically dead. I knew it, I knew I was dead and I heard all those machines fighting for my life.'

'And then?'

'And then I thought: I want to live. When I came round from the anaesthetic I knew my legs had been amputated, even though the nurses didn't want to tell me. But I was thinking: "I have lost my legs but not my will to live", and that is far more important.'

'And what do you want to do now?'

'When I'm better I'll go back to school. I was doing a confectionary course at college. I'd like to work there.'

His parents arrived, holding tightly on to each other. The mother seemed to be supporting the father. Avdo proudly showed them his chocolate and oranges. Before leaving I took a photograph of him with his parents.

A few flakes of snow started to fall as I was walking back from the hospital. Reuter's armoured car stopped and offered me a lift. I said I preferred to walk.

I was tired of driving about in cars with my heart in my mouth, tired of racing flat out down the ramp into the Holiday Inn car park, tired of dodging from one side of a cross-roads to another thinking about the sniper taking aim with his rifle. I was tired of never being able to look out of a window, day or night, because those bastards have infrared sights. I was tired of warily watching Mount Trebevic, of sleeping fully dressed, of never washing, of being cold.

It had been less than a month, but I was tired. I wanted, just for once, to walk, and if some damned bullet got me, so be it! The men in the mountains could register a victory as far as I was concerned.

I was wearing a safety helmet and bullet-proof jacket. The people in the streets, the others, didn't have such things. They had heavy bags and were dragging firewood and dustbins filled with water.

They had been doing so for eight months.

I was about to return to Italy, but at that moment it hardly mattered. I was not even sure that I was still alive. After a while, the distinction between life and death becomes blurred in Sarajevo.

It was cold walking down the hill. I stopped in front of a once-glazed door wondering if this were a public building. It looked like a timber warehouse but there was a long counter, like a bar, at the far end. Two women, sitting beside a cast-iron stove on which a small saucepan was steaming, beckoned me in. I sat down at a small table, took off my helmet and lit a cigarette. The women were watching me, so I offered them one, and when they accepted with alacrity I gave them the whole packet.

Three men came in. A transistor radio was playing a popular song. I tried to remember the title: it was Elton John's Nikita.

The women took the saucepan off the stove, emptied it into a plate and put it on the table in front of me, inviting me to eat. I ate, alone, while the others watched in silence. As I left, they said: 'VRATI SE. Come back again.'

Here and there on the battered, smoke-blackened walls was written in large, plain letters, in English: PLEASE HELP BOSNIA NOW!

Back at the hotel I met Ademir on the stairs. He asked me:
'*Will you come back to Sarajevo?*'

'*I don't know, but I believe I shall do all I can.*'

From his jacket pocket he pulled out the biro he always used.
'*Here, have this. Take it back with you.*'

'*What about the film?*' *I asked him.* '*When do you start shooting?*'

'*We've not been able to make a start yet. We've had to put it back.*'

'*What will you do meanwhile?*'

'*For the moment I shall try to do some television work. In June, to keep people's spirits up, I made a video. I shot it in the Olympic Stadium the day it was destroyed by bombs. We were up to our ankles in water and mud, and a Sarajevo group stood in the rubble and sang* 'Help Bosnia now!' *The music, I must say, was very beautiful.*'

'*So that explains the appearance of those words all over the city. It was for your video.*'

'*Yes. But if I were to do another video now, I would write something different.*'

'*Like what?*'

'*I would say:* WORLD HELP YOURSELF NOW, *because by abandoning Sarajevo to its fate you have signalled that you have abandoned all faith in yourself.*'